AFTERNOON TEA
AT THE
cutter & squidge
BAKERY

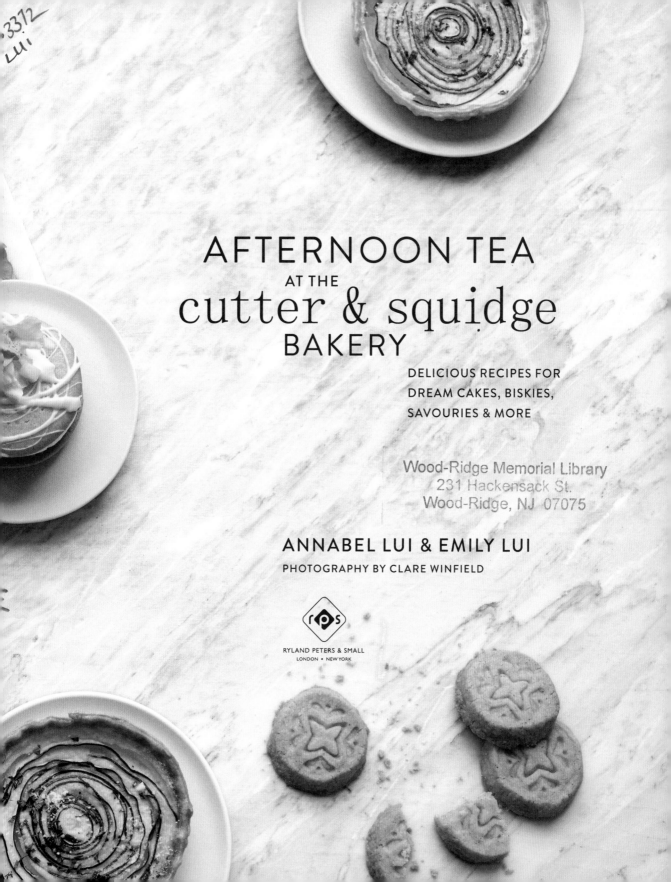

AFTERNOON TEA
AT THE
cutter & squidge
BAKERY

DELICIOUS RECIPES FOR
DREAM CAKES, BISKIES,
SAVOURIES & MORE

ANNABEL LUI & EMILY LUI
PHOTOGRAPHY BY CLARE WINFIELD

RYLAND PETERS & SMALL
LONDON • NEW YORK

DEDICATION

To Coco, our mascot, you were smart, sassy and determined; all the essential female qualities.

To our family and loved ones who have all been supportive, patient and understanding, enabling us to create and grow Cutter & Squidge into what it is today, and what it will be in the future.

Senior Designer Megan Smith
Commissioning Editor Alice Sambrook
Production David Hearn
Art Director Leslie Harrington
Editorial Director Julia Charles
Publisher Cindy Richards

Food Stylist Tamara Vos
Prop Stylist Alexander Breeze
Illustration Rebecca Rank
Indexer Hilary Bird

First published in 2019 by
Ryland Peters & Small
20–21 Jockey's Fields
London WC1R 4BW
and
341 East 116th Street
New York, NY 10029
www.rylandpeters.com

10 9 8 7 6 5 4 3 2 1

All photography by Clare Winfield except page 7 by Richard Fairclough.

ISBN: 978-1-78879-158-8

CIP data from the Library of Congress has been applied for. A CIP record for this book is available from the British Library.

COOK'S NOTES

· Both British (metric) and American (Imperial plus US cups) measurements are included in these recipes; however, it is important to work with one set of measurements and not alternate between the two within a recipe.

· All eggs are medium (UK) or large (US), unless otherwise specified.

· For best results, all eggs should be used at room temperature. We have included this information in some recipes where it is vital as a helpful reminder.

· When a recipe calls for the grated zest of citrus fruit, buy unwaxed fruit and wash well before use. If you can only find treated fruit, scrub well in warm soapy water and rinse before using.

· For the best flavour, we recommend using vanilla bean paste, but if you can't find this, then use the same quantity of vanilla extract instead.

contents

introduction

Writing this book has been both a trip down memory lane, revisiting some of our favourite flavour combinations from over the years, and an exciting opportunity for us to create some completely new, delicious bakes, just for you.

We were first inspired to create Cutter & Squidge after feeling perplexed that the baking world insisted on using bottled food colourings and synthetic flavourings, and wondering why everyone made the same products. We realized that there might be a gap in the market for something different, and from that day, our mission became to create something new that would satisfy both of our cravings. For Annabel – chewy brownies, crunchy, crisp biscuits and soft cookies, and for Emily – cake – any cake! The biskie was then born – two chewy cookie-cake hybrids sandwiching a light, moussey buttercream packed with delicious flavours. Our name also came from the creation of the biskie, when one of us would cut out the dough and the other would squidge it together!

We spent an initial 10 months developing our first recipes to get them just right. Using natural ingredients has always been important to us; in our minds, if we are making something in a particular flavour, then it should actually contain that ingredient rather than an artificial version. We like to celebrate natural beauty, and to us, there is nothing more beautiful than natural colours. We wanted to share with you how easy it is to create an amazing array of colours using natural ingredients, so turn to page 8 to read more about this.

Our repertoire of recipes is a reflection of our oriental heritage mixed with our family's passion for classic British and French baking. Our father was locally famous for his lemon meringue pies, apple pies and melt-in-the-mouth choux profiteroles – he still makes them now for family gatherings and we LOVE them. The crazy work ethic that our parents instilled in us provided us with the energy and focus to take the first Cutter & Squidge biskie from a Saturday food market at Duke of York Square in Chelsea, to Selfridges and Harrods, to opening a pop-up store, to our first permanent store and café on Brewer Street, Soho, and a second store in the City of London. It has been quite a journey, and as we have grown Cutter & Squidge, we have been lucky enough to work with some amazingly creative and like-minded people, who are also passionate about delicious, all-natural products.

Our Soho store is where we first launched our famous afternoon teas. These began with our signature afternoon tea served in Chinese steam baskets; then came an exciting collaboration with Sanrio to host the first Hello Kitty food concept in Europe – Hello Kitty's Secret Garden Afternoon Tea. We then created a jewel-encrusted, glittering genie's cave from the Aladdin fairy tale for our Genie's Cave Afternoon Tea. After this, a castle dungeon became the setting for our immersive Potion Room Afternoon Tea, complete with a potions master teacher, magical bakes and drinkable potions.

Our afternoon teas give us the opportunity to push our creativity and to create exciting, unique bakes in addition to our staple biskies and dream cakes, and this book enables us to share our favourites with you. We want you to have fun making, sharing and eating the recipes in this book! They range from easy cookies, traybakes and pastries to the slightly trickier layer cakes and our signature biskies. Everything has been written to help you achieve the best results at home – we started Cutter & Squidge from our home kitchen, so it makes sense that you can create our bakes from yours! We have split the book into themes, but we encourage you to mix and match any recipes that catch your imagination to create your own unique and delicious afternoon tea.

natural food colourings

Bottled food colourings often leave an unpleasant aftertaste and the chemicals may not be very healthy, either. We have found that we can achieve a stunning rainbow of colours using plant-based ingredients, many of which are now readily available in supermarkets or health food stores. They generally won't be as bright as E-number-based colourings, instead they give the natural hues you see throughout this book.

Below are some tips to remember when using natural colourings and a rundown of some of the key ingredients:

1. We usually mix powders with a little water to make a paste before adding to recipes, as this gives a stronger colour.

2. Some natural food colours are not 'bake stable', which means that at high temperatures they turn brown or dull. We mostly keep our sponges natural and save the colours for decoration.

3. Due to the natural chemicals in berries, they react to pH levels. If you add lemon juice (acid) to raspberry it will turn pinker. If you add bicarbonate of soda/baking soda (alkaline) it will turn blue-green.

TURMERIC (YELLOW) A root spice with an astringent taste, you'll be able to taste it if you use too much. Use sparingly as the colour of turmeric develops over time.

CARROT (ORANGE) This must be hydrated with water before use. It will give you a lovely orange hue and can be mixed with turmeric or beetroot/beet powder to make peach or coral. It adds little flavour.

STRAWBERRY (RED) This gives an intense strawberry milkshake colour and a nice, almost sharp, strawberry flavour which balances out sweetness.

RASPBERRY (FUCHSIA PINK) Raspberry powder mixed with a little water will give an intense pink or a paler pink if mixed with buttercream. Its sharp, fruity flavour also helps to balance sweetness.

BEETROOT (RED/PINK) Gives a deep pink/red colour, which leaves little taste. We also bake this in our Red Velvet Cup Cakes and Pink Thumbprint Cookies.

BLUEBERRY (PURPLE) Blueberry powder creates a pretty lilac/purple colour (without much taste), which is stronger when added to light/white buttercream.

GREEN SPIRULINA (FOREST/MINT GREEN) Gives a dark forest green or a cool mint green when added to white. It can taste like seaweed if you add too much.

MATCHA (GREEN) A ground Japanese green tea that gives a vibrant green colour to buttercream or a darker colour and a unique flavour to cookies or cake.

BLUE SPIRULINA (BLUE) Part of the algae family, this makes everything from electric blue to baby blue. It tastes a little, but is hidden with a dash of vanilla.

CINNAMON (LIGHT BROWN) Gives a light toffee brown colour but also a strong flavour, so use accordingly.

ACTIVATED CHARCOAL (GREY/BLACK) Can colour anything black or any shade of grey. It is relatively tasteless.

COCOA (BROWN) Used sparingly, this can give a light brown colour, but will taste more chocolatey the more you add.

TURMERIC

STRAWBERRY

RASPBERRY

CARROT

GREEN SPIRULINA

MATCHA

BEETROOT/BEET

BLUE SPIRULINA

CHARCOAL

COCOA

BLUEBERRY

CINNAMON

BASIC
RECIPES

SPONGES

Our fluffy but moist sponge recipes are based on a traditional recipe from the north of England. You can swap the vanilla bean paste for lemon zest or almond extract for a flavour variation.

vanilla cake batter

15-CM/6-INCH CAKE

175 g/1½ sticks unsalted butter, softened
175 g/¾ cup plus 2 tablespoons caster/
  granulated sugar
4 eggs, at room temperature
1 teaspoon vanilla bean paste
240 g/1¾ cups plain/all-purpose flour
1 teaspoon baking powder
85 ml/⅓ cup buttermilk, at room temperature
1 teaspoon bicarbonate of soda/baking soda

Preheat the oven to 180°C/fan 160°C (350°F) Gas 4.

Put the softened butter, sugar, eggs and vanilla paste in a mixing bowl. Sift in the flour and the baking powder and mix with a hand-held electric whisk (or use a stand mixer with the paddle attachment), starting at a slow speed and then progressing to medium, for about 1 minute until well combined, scraping down the bowl a couple of times.

In a separate bowl, mix the buttermilk and bicarbonate of soda/baking soda together until foamy and quickly add to the cake batter. Mix at a medium-high speed until combined; do not overmix or the sponge will be tough.

Divide the cake batter into the pans specified in the recipe and bake in the preheated oven for 20–25 minutes for three pans or 30–35 minutes for two pans until golden and springy to the touch.

20-CM/8-INCH CAKE

250 g/2¼ sticks unsalted butter, softened
250 g/1¼ cups caster/granulated sugar
6 eggs, at room temperature
2 teaspoons vanilla bean paste
340 g/2½ cups plain/all-purpose flour
2 teaspoons baking powder
120 ml/½ cup buttermilk, at room temperature
2 teaspoons bicarbonate of soda/baking soda

Preheat the oven to 180°C/fan 160°C (350°F) Gas 4.

Put the softened butter, sugar, eggs and vanilla paste in a mixing bowl. Sift in the flour and the baking powder and mix with a hand-held electric whisk (or use a stand mixer with the paddle attachment), starting at a slow speed and then progressing to medium, for about 1 minute until well combined, scraping down the bowl a couple of times.

In a separate bowl, mix the buttermilk and bicarbonate of soda/baking soda together until foamy and quickly add to the cake batter. Mix at a medium-high speed until combined; do not overmix or the sponge will be tough.

Divide the cake batter into the pans specified in the recipe and bake in the preheated oven for 25–30 minutes for three pans or 35–40 minutes for two pans until golden and springy to the touch.

chocolate cake batter

15-CM/6-INCH CAKE

175 g/1½ sticks unsalted butter, softened
175 g/¾ cup plus 2 tablespoons caster/
   granulated sugar
4 eggs, at room temperature
200 g/1½ cups plain/all-purpose flour
40 g/½ cup cocoa powder
1 teaspoon baking powder
85 ml/⅓ cup buttermilk, at room temperature
1 teaspoon bicarbonate of soda/baking soda

Preheat the oven to 180°C/fan 160°C
(350°F) Gas 4.

   Put the softened butter, sugar and eggs
in a mixing bowl. Sift in the flour, cocoa and
baking powder and mix with a hand-held
electric whisk (or use a stand mixer with the
paddle attachment), starting slow and then at
a medium speed, for about 1 minute, scraping
down the sides of the bowl a couple of times.

   In a separate bowl, mix the buttermilk and
bicarbonate of soda/baking soda together until
foamy and quickly add to the cake batter.
Mix at a medium-high speed until combined;
do not overmix or the sponge will be tough.

   Divide the cake batter into the pans
specified in the recipe and bake in the
preheated oven for 20–25 minutes for three
pans or 30–35 minutes for two pans until
springy to the touch.

20-CM/8-INCH CAKE

250 g/2¼ sticks unsalted butter, softened
250 g/1¼ cups caster/granulated sugar
6 eggs, at room temperature
265 g/2 cups plain/all-purpose flour
75 g/¾ cup cocoa powder
2 teaspoons baking powder
120 ml/½ cup buttermilk, at room temperature
2 teaspoons bicarbonate of soda/baking soda

Preheat the oven to 180°C/fan 160°C
(350°F) Gas 4.

   Put the softened butter, sugar and eggs
in a mixing bowl. Sift in the flour, cocoa and
baking powder and mix with a hand-held
electric whisk (or use a stand mixer with the
paddle attachment), starting slow and then at
a medium speed, for about 1 minute, scraping
down the sides of the bowl a couple of times.

   In a separate bowl, mix the buttermilk and
bicarbonate of soda/baking soda together until
foamy and quickly add to the cake batter.
Mix at a medium-high speed until combined;
do not overmix or the sponge will be tough.

   Divide the cake batter into the pans
specified in the recipe and bake in the
preheated oven for 25–30 minutes for three
pans or 35–40 minutes for two pans until
springy to the touch.

CRUMBS

These crumbs are little pebbles of magic, they have multiple uses in our recipes and provide a great texture to elevate your bakes. You can leave them out, but the results just won't be the same! If a recipe calls for a smaller amount, you can halve the ingredients or save the rest for another recipe.

digestive

125 g/1⅛ sticks unsalted butter, melted
250 g/1¾ cups plus 2 tablespoons plain/all-purpose flour
60 g/⅓ cup minus 1 teaspoon caster/granulated sugar
60 g/⅓ cup minus 1 teaspoon soft light brown sugar
2½ teaspoons salt

MAKES ABOUT 450 G/16 OZ.

Preheat the oven to 190°C/fan 170°C (375°F) Gas 5.

Mix together all the ingredients by hand in a bowl until resembling fine breadcrumbs. Tip onto a baking sheet lined with greaseproof baking parchment and bake in the preheated oven for 15–20 minutes until lightly golden. Fork through the mixture as it cools to create fine crumbs.

Store in an airtight container for up to 2 weeks or in the freezer for up to 3 months.

chocolate

100 g/1 stick minus 1 tablespoon unsalted butter, melted
120 g/1 cup minus 1½ tablespoons plain/all-purpose flour
110 g/½ cup plus 1 tablespoon caster/granulated sugar
70 g/scant ¾ cup cornflour/cornstarch
50 g/½ cup cocoa powder

MAKES ABOUT 450 G/16 OZ.

Preheat the oven to 180°C/fan 160°C (350°F) Gas 4.

Mix together all the ingredients by hand in a bowl until resembling fine breadcrumbs. Tip onto a baking sheet lined with greaseproof baking parchment and bake in the preheated oven for 20 minutes until pale but cooked. Fork through the mixture as it cools to create fine crumbs.

Store in an airtight container for up to 2 weeks or in the freezer for up to 1 month.

vanilla

100 g/1 stick minus 1 tablespoon unsalted butter, melted
170 g/1¼ cups plain/all-purpose flour
110 g/½ cup plus 1 tablespoon caster/granulated sugar
70 g/¾ cup cornflour/cornstarch
1 teaspoon vanilla extract

MAKES ABOUT 450 G/16 OZ.

Preheat the oven to 180°C/fan 160°C (350°F) Gas 4.

Mix together all the ingredients by hand in a bowl until resembling fine breadcrumbs. Tip onto a baking sheet lined with greaseproof baking parchment and bake in the preheated oven for 20 minutes until pale but cooked. Fork through the mixture as it cools to create fine crumbs.

Store in an airtight container for up to 2 weeks or in the freezer for up to 1 month.

PASTRY

Our pastry recipes are super simple and don't take much effort. Puff pastry can be scary but our vegan rough puff pastry is a must try for all vegans and non-vegans alike; the coconut oil gives a crisp, light pastry which tastes divine.

sweet shortcrust

270 g/2 cups plain/all-purpose flour
90 g/scant ½ cup caster/granulated sugar
120 g/1⅛ sticks cold unsalted butter, cubed
1 UK large/US extra-large egg

MAKES ABOUT 600 G/21 OZ.

Sift the flour into a mixing bowl and stir in the sugar. Rub in the cold cubed butter with your fingertips until the mixture resembles fine breadcrumbs.

Stir in the egg and bring the mixture together into a dough. Form into a ball with your hands, then wrap in clingfilm/plastic wrap and chill in the fridge for at least 15 minutes.

After resting, use the pastry according to the recipe. Your pastry may be too firm to roll out straight from the fridge, so leave it at room temperature for 10 minutes to warm and soften slightly before using.

rough puff

125 g/1 cup minus
1 tablespoon plain/
all-purpose flour,
plus extra for
dusting the work
surface
½ teaspoon fine sea
salt

125 g/1⅛ sticks room
temperature
unsalted butter
(not too soft),
cubed
75 ml/⅓ cup cold
water

**MAKES ABOUT
350 G/12 OZ.**

Sift the flour and salt into a mixing bowl
and mix together. Roughly rub the butter into
the flour, stopping when there are still large
butterbean-sized lumps of butter visible.

Make a well in the middle of the mixture
and add about three quarters of the cold water.
Mix to bring the dough together, only adding
the remaining water if needed. Form the
dough into a ball, wrap in clingfilm/plastic
wrap and rest in the fridge for 20 minutes.

Remove the wrapping and gently knead
through; you will see marbling from the lumps
of butter. Pat the dough into a rectangular
shape. Lightly flour the work surface and
rolling pin and place the dough with the short
side nearest you. Roll the pastry out in one
direction (without turning) until it is approx.
20 x 5-cm/8 x 2-inches. Fold the top third
inwards, then the bottom third over the top
of this (this is called laminating or creating
the flaky layers). Give the pastry a quarter
turn, then repeat the rolling and folding.
Repeat the quarter turn, rolling and folding
once more. Your pastry is now ready to use.
Wrap and refrigerate if not using immediately
or if it has become sticky.

vegan rough puff

125 g/1 cup minus
1 tablespoon plain/
all-purpose flour,
plus extra for
dusting the work
surface
½ teaspoon fine sea
salt

100 g/3½ oz. coconut
oil, at room
temperature
(but not too soft),
roughly cut up
75 ml/⅓ cup cold
water

**MAKES ABOUT
350 G/12 OZ.**

Sift the flour and salt into a mixing bowl and
mix together. Roughly rub the coconut oil into
the flour, stopping when there are still large
pea/bean-sized lumps of coconut oil visible.

Make a well in the middle of the mixture
and add about three quarters of the cold water.
Mix to bring the dough together, only adding
the remaining water if needed. Form the
dough into a ball, wrap in clingfilm/plastic
wrap and rest in the fridge for 20 minutes.

Remove the plastic and gently knead; you
will see marbling from the coconut oil lumps.
If the lumps break through the dough they
are too cold, so knead a little longer. Pat it into
a rectangular shape. Lightly flour the work
surface and rolling pin and place the dough
with the short side nearest you. Roll the pastry
out in one direction (without turning) until it is
approx. 20 x 5-cm/8 x 2-inches. Fold the top
third inwards, then the bottom third over the
top of this (this is called laminating). Give the
pastry a quarter turn, then repeat the rolling
and folding. Repeat the quarter turn, rolling
and folding once more. Your pastry is now
ready to use. Wrap and refrigerate if not using
immediately or if it has become sticky.

BUTTERCREAMS & CUSTARDS

These buttercreams are so special to us! We have spent a long time
perfecting these recipes so that they are light, creamy and full of favour.

light as a feather cake buttercream

6 egg whites
260 g/1¼ cups caster/granulated sugar
430 g/4 sticks unsalted butter, softened
1 teaspoon vanilla bean paste

MAKES ABOUT 900 G/2 LB.

Stir together the egg whites and sugar in
a heatproof bowl. Place over a pan of gently
simmering water (making sure that the
base of the bowl does not touch the water).
Heat gently, stirring occasionally, for about
20 minutes or until the sugar has dissolved.
You can check this by rubbing some between
your fingertips – it should not be grainy.

Remove the bowl from the pan and use
a hand-held electric whisk (or a stand mixer
with a whisk attachment) to whisk for about
10–15 minutes until cool with stiff peaks.

Add the softened butter and whisk for
a further 5–7 minutes until light cream in
colour. Stir in the vanilla paste. It should have
the consistency of medium-soft whipped
cream, and be very easy to pipe and spread.

TIP If your buttercream splits, freeze it until
frozen solid. Melt a quarter in the microwave
until liquid, then whisk back into the frozen
buttercream until it comes back together.

biskie buttercream

ROUX
300 ml/1¼ cups
    whole milk
60 g/generous
    ½ cup cornflour/
    cornstarch

TO FINISH
360 g/3¼ sticks cold
    unsalted butter
90 g/scant ½ cup
    caster/granulated
    sugar

**MAKES ABOUT
800 G/1¾ LB.**

To make the roux, put the milk into a saucepan
over a medium heat until steaming.

Meanwhile, mix the cornflour/cornstarch
with 100 ml/⅓ cup plus 1 tablespoon cold
water. Add this to the steaming milk and whisk
vigorously! Heat, stirring continuously, for
2–3 minutes until the roux is bubbling a little
and thickened and the cornflour/cornstarch
has cooked out. Pour the roux into a shallow
dish or tray. Pop clingfilm/plastic wrap on top
and let it cool and solidify.

To finish the buttercream, put the cold
butter and sugar into a mixing bowl. Add the
cold solidified roux and beat with a hand-held
electric whisk (or use a stand mixer with the
paddle attachment). The mixture will start to
break up and look split and slushy, but keep
beating for 4–6 minutes, scraping down the
sides of the bowl occasionally. The buttercream
will turn into something that resembles whipped
double/heavy cream, but be sure not to
overmix as it can split.

coconut ganache

400 ml/scant 1¾ cups full-fat
   coconut milk
50 g/½ cup cornflour/cornstarch
200 g/7 oz. white chocolate,
   broken into pieces

MAKES ABOUT 500 G/18 OZ.

Combine the coconut milk
and cornflour/cornstarch in a
saucepan and mix really well,
so that no lumps remain. Place
the pan over a medium-low heat
and stir continuously for about
5–10 minutes as the mixture
gently bubbles and thickens,
like a white sauce.

Pour the hot, thick coconut
mixture over the white
chocolate in a bowl and mix to
melt the chocolate and combine
into a smooth ganache. Leave to
cool, then transfer to an airtight
container in the fridge.

Once cooled, the ganache
should be nice and spreadable,
but if it is too hard, then
microwave in 20-second bursts
until spreadable.

Put in a bowl and cover
directly with clingfilm/plastic
wrap and refrigerate for 1 hour
before using. It will keep for up
to 1 week.

chocolate custard

85 g/scant ½ cup caster/
   granulated sugar
20 g/scant ¼ cup cornflour/
   cornstarch
1 egg yolk
225 ml/scant 1 cup whole milk
70 ml/scant ⅓ cup double/heavy
   cream
35 g/scant ⅓ cup cocoa powder
85 g/3 oz. dark/bittersweet
   chocolate, broken into pieces
85 g/3 oz. milk chocolate,
   broken into pieces
35 g/¼ stick unsalted butter

MAKES ABOUT 500 G/18 OZ.

Mix together the sugar and
cornflour/cornstarch in a
bowl. Add the egg yolk but
do not mix in. Set aside.

Stir together the milk,
cream and cocoa powder in
a saucepan and heat until
steaming. Pour the cream slowly
over the cornflour/cornstarch
and yolk, whisking to combine.

Return to the saucepan over
a low heat for 8–10 minutes,
stirring, until thickened. Add
both types of chocolate and
the butter and mix until melted.

Put in a bowl and cover
directly with clingfilm/plastic
wrap and refrigerate for 1 hour
before using. It will keep for up
to 1 week.

cream cheese custard

100 ml/⅓ cup plus 1 tablespoon
   double/heavy cream
20 g/scant ¼ cup cornflour/
   cornstarch
2 eggs
100 g/3½ oz. white chocolate,
   broken into pieces
100 g/scant ½ cup full-fat
   cream cheese

MAKES ABOUT 300 G/10½ OZ.

Combine the double/heavy
cream and cornflour/cornstarch
in a saucepan and whisk
together until smooth. Add
the eggs and whisk in until fully
combined. Place the saucepan
over a low-medium heat and
cook for about 10–12 minutes,
whisking, until thickened.
Remove from the heat.

Melt the white chocolate in
the microwave in short bursts.
Combine the thickened cream
mixture and melted white
chocolate in a bowl with the
cream cheese and whisk until
fully combined. Transfer the
custard to a bowl and cover
the top directly with clingfilm/
plastic wrap and refrigerate for
1 hour before using. It will keep
for up to 1 week.

SYRUPS & SOAKS

A flavoured syrup will take your baking from tasty to divine! These are very important as they are one of the key ways in which we naturally add flavour to our bakes. All syrups and soaks will keep in the fridge for up to 1 week.

vanilla syrup

200 g/1 cup caster/granulated sugar
10 g/¼ oz. vanilla bean paste

MAKES ABOUT 400 ML/ SCANT 1¾ CUPS

Stir together the sugar and vanilla in a saucepan with 200 ml/generous ¾ cup water. Bring to the boil, then remove from the heat. Use warm.

chocolate syrup

200 g/1 cup caster/granulated sugar
20 g/scant ¼ cup cocoa powder

MAKES ABOUT 400 ML/ SCANT 1¾ CUPS

Stir together the sugar and cocoa powder in a saucepan with 200 ml/generous ¾ cup water. Bring just to the boil, then remove from the heat. Use the syrup warm.

lemon soak

40 ml/3 tablespoons freshly squeezed lemon juice (about 2 lemons)
200 g/1 cup caster/ granulated sugar

MAKES ABOUT 400 ML/ SCANT 1¾ CUPS

Stir together the lemon juice and sugar in a saucepan with 160 ml/⅔ cup water. Bring just to the boil, then remove from the heat. Use the soak warm.

passion fruit syrup

6 passion fruits
100 g/½ cup caster/granulated sugar

MAKES ABOUT 300 ML/1¼ CUPS

Halve the passion fruits, scoop out the flesh and sieve/strain to remove the seeds. Stir together the juice and sugar in a pan and heat gently until the sugar has dissolved. Leave the syrup to cool before using.

coconut soak

100 g/½ cup caster/granulated sugar
400 ml/scant 1¾ cups coconut milk

MAKES ABOUT 400 ML/ SCANT 1¾ CUPS

Stir together the sugar and coconut milk in a saucepan. Heat gently until warm to the touch and the sugar has dissolved. Use the soak warm.

JAMS & CURDS

Our homemade jams and curds are made using less sugar than shop-bought versions, and contain no additives. This ensures our bakes have a good balance of sugar and tartness, and lets the natural flavours come through.

strawberry jam

400 g/14 oz. frozen strawberries
100 g/½ cup caster/granulated
  sugar
12 g/3 level teaspoons pectin
  powder
small squeeze of fresh lemon
  juice

MAKES ABOUT 450 G/1 LB.

Stir together all the ingredients
in a saucepan and simmer over
a low-medium heat for about
10 minutes, stirring, until the
fruit has broken down and the
jam is thick. Leave to cool. It will
keep in the fridge for up to
2–3 weeks.

raspberry jam

400 g/14 oz. frozen raspberries
100 g/½ cup caster/granulated
  sugar
12 g/3 level teaspoons pectin
  powder
small squeeze of fresh lemon
  juice

MAKES ABOUT 450 G/1 LB.

Stir together all the ingredients
in a saucepan and simmer over
a low-medium heat for about
10 minutes, stirring, until the
fruit has broken down and the
jam is thick. If you don't want
the seeds you can pass the jam
through a sieve/strainer. Leave
to cool. It will keep in the fridge
for up to 2–3 weeks.

lemon curd

2 egg yolks
75 g/⅓ cup plus 2 teaspoons
  caster/granulated sugar
5 g/1 teaspoon pectin powder
40 g/3 tablespoons unsalted
  butter, cubed
150 ml/⅔ cup freshly squeezed
  lemon juice

MAKES ABOUT 300 G/10½ OZ.

Combine all the ingredients
in a heatproof bowl.

  Place the bowl over a pan
of barely simmering water,
whisking every 10 minutes,
for about 30-40 minutes until
well combined and thickened.

  Transfer the curd to an
airtight container. Whisk as
it cools to prevent a skin from
forming. It will keep in the
fridge for up to 2–3 weeks.

blueberry jam

300 g/10½ oz. fresh or frozen
  blueberries
150 g/¾ cup caster/granulated
  sugar

MAKES ABOUT 450 G/1 LB.

Stir together the ingredients
in a saucepan with 60 ml/¼ cup
water. Bring to a simmer over
a low-medium heat for about
3-5 minutes until the berries
have released their juices. Leave
to cool. It will keep in the fridge
for up to 2–3 weeks.

apple jam

2 large Bramley apples (300 g/
  10½ oz.) or other cooking
  apples that break down easily,
  peeled, cored and chopped
100 g/½ cup soft light brown
  sugar

MAKES ABOUT 350 G/12 OZ.

Stir together all the ingredients
in a saucepan and simmer
over a low-medium heat for
10 minutes until the apples
are mushy and the jam is thick.
Leave to cool. It will keep in the
fridge for up to 2–3 weeks.

CARAMELS

Don't be scared of making caramel! We take our caramels a little darker than normal, which results in a stronger taste that everyone loves. You can drizzle these caramels on anything from ice cream to toast.

caramel sauce

250 g/1¼ cups caster/
    granulated sugar
250 ml/generous 1 cup double/
    heavy cream
25 g/1¼ tablespoons golden/
    light corn syrup
15 g/1 tablespoon unsalted
    butter

MAKES ABOUT 500 G/18 OZ.

Add the sugar to a warmed saucepan and melt over a medium heat until liquid and a light caramel colour.

Whisk in the cream and then the golden/light corn syrup; it will bubble, so be careful and whisk quickly until all combined.

Finally, add the butter and stir until melted.

Leave to cool and then the caramel is ready to use. Store in a sealed jar in the fridge, where it will keep for up to 2 months.

salted caramel sauce

250 g/1¼ cups caster/
    granulated sugar
250 g/generous 1 cup double/
    heavy cream
25 g/1¼ tablespoons golden/
    light corn syrup
15 g/1 tablespoon unsalted
    butter
8 g/2 teaspoons Maldon sea salt
    flakes

MAKES ABOUT 500 G/18 OZ.

Add the sugar to a warmed saucepan and melt over a medium heat until liquid and a light caramel colour.

Whisk in the cream and then the golden/light corn syrup; it will bubble so be careful and whisk quickly until combined.

Finally, add the butter and salt and stir until melted.

Once cool, it is ready to use. Store in an airtight container or a jar in the fridge, where it will keep for up to 2 months.

butterscotch sauce

200 g/1 cup dark brown
    soft sugar
20g/1 tablespoon golden/
    light corn syrup
75 ml/⅓ cup double/heavy
    cream
½ teaspoon fine salt
25 g/1¾ tablespoons unsalted
    butter

MAKES ABOUT 350 G/12 OZ.

Stir together the soft dark brown sugar in a saucepan with 50 ml/3½ tablespoons water and the golden/light corn syrup. Set over a medium heat until boiling.

Stir in the cream, salt and butter. Boil for a further 10 minutes, without stirring, until the butterscotch sauce is glossy and thick enough to coat the back of a spoon.

Leave to cool and then use as desired. It will keep for up to 1 week in the fridge.

SIGNATURE
afternoon tea

This chapter features some Cutter & Squidge best sellers as well as other guaranteed crowd-pleasers. Here you will find our trademark mix of British and oriental flavours, showcased in some of our signature bakes and drinks.

smoked cheese & black pepper scones

Smoked cheese, Parmesan and black pepper provide a delicious savoury twist on this afternoon tea staple. Serve these scones simply warm and buttered, or with smoked salmon, cress and cream cheese.

DIFFICULTY	MAKES 16–18 SCONES	PREP TIME 30 MINUTES	BAKE TIME 15 MINUTES

500 g/3¾ cups plain/
  all-purpose flour, plus extra
  for dusting
1 tablespoon bicarbonate of soda/
  baking soda
¼ teaspoon cracked black pepper,
  plus extra for sprinkling on top
250 g/2¼ sticks unsalted butter,
  chilled
175 g/6 oz. grated smoked
  Cheddar cheese
50 g/1¾ oz. finely grated
  Parmesan cheese
75 ml/⅓ cup warm whole milk
1 egg, plus 1 beaten egg for
  brushing

5-cm/2-inch round cookie cutter

Preheat the oven to 220°C/fan 200°C (425°F) Gas 7.

Sift the flour and bicarbonate of soda/baking soda together into a mixing bowl and add the cracked black pepper.

Cut the cold butter into cubes and rub with your fingertips into the flour mixture until it resembles fine breadcrumbs.

Add 125 g/4½ oz. of the grated smoked Cheddar cheese and all the grated Parmesan and mix in.

Add the warm milk and egg and mix until combined. The mixture should be soft and sticky.

On a lightly floured surface, roll the mixture out to a thickness of about 2.5 cm/1 inch. Use the round cutter to stamp out rounds but DO NOT TWIST as you cut! Just pull straight up.

Space the scones out over two non-stick baking sheets and brush with the beaten egg. Sprinkle over some extra cracked black pepper and scatter over the remaining grated smoked Cheddar cheese.

Bake in the preheated oven for 15 minutes until the scones are lightly brown and have puffed up. Remove from the oven and leave to cool.

Serve with fillings of your choice. The scones will keep for up to 3 days in an airtight container.

cheese clouds

These light and savoury cheese chouquettes are so moreish – a batch of 40 will disappear in no time! They are perfect served warm with a homemade tomato sauce or cool and filled with whipped goat's cheese.

DIFFICULTY 🥄🥄🥄 | **MAKES 40** | **PREP TIME 25 MINUTES** | **BAKE TIME 25 MINUTES**

125 g/1⅛ sticks unsalted butter
½ teaspoon fine salt
¼ teaspoon freshly ground black pepper
250 g/1¾ cups plus 2 tablespoons plain/all-purpose flour
7 eggs
250 g/9 oz. grated mozzarella cheese
20 g/¾ oz. finely grated Parmesan cheese
25 g/¾ oz. finely chopped fresh parsley

TO SERVE (OPTIONAL)
homemade tomato sauce
  or whipped goat's cheese

*piping/pastry bag with a 2-cm/
  ¾-inch plain nozzle/tip*
*2 baking sheets, lined with
  greaseproof baking parchment*

Put the butter, salt and pepper and 340 ml/scant 1½ cups water into a non-stick saucepan over a medium heat. Heat until the butter has melted and the mixture is simmering, then remove the pan from the heat and quickly add all the flour in one go. Place the pan back over a low-medium heat and stir briskly with a wooden spoon for about 3–5 minutes until the mixture forms a firm dough. Transfer the dough to a mixing bowl and leave for 2 minutes to cool down a little.

Add the eggs, one at a time, and use a wooden spoon (or the paddle attachment in a stand mixer) to beat in after each addition, until the mixture is smooth and thick. Add the grated mozzarella, the grated Parmesan and the chopped parsley and stir to evenly combine them with the dough. Leave the mixture to cool completely.

Preheat the oven to 220°C/fan 200°C (425°F) Gas 7.

Place the dough into the piping/pastry bag with the 2-cm/ ¾-inch nozzle/tip and pipe ten 3-cm/1¼-inch round blobs onto each prepared baking sheet, leaving a 3-cm/1¼-inch gap either side for expansion. Bake in the preheated oven for 25 minutes, until the puffs are golden brown. Repeat for the remaining mixture and bake the next batch – you should be able to make 40 in total.

These are best enjoyed warm but are still tasty cold.

Mini sweetcorn pancakes

There are two ways to cook these scrumptious mini pancakes: gently fried for a soft finish with lightly browned edges, or quickly shallow-fried for a crispy, crunchy outer finish. Try both and let us know which you prefer!

DIFFICULTY | **MAKES APPROX. 6** | **PREP TIME** 10 MINUTES | **COOK TIME** 10 MINUTES

100 g/¾ cup plain/
   all-purpose flour
½ teaspoon baking powder
2 pinches fine salt
2 pinches freshly ground black
   pepper
1 pinch dried chilli flakes/hot red
   pepper flakes
265 g/9 oz. well-drained canned
   sweetcorn/corn, dried on a
   paper towel
1 tablespoon extra-virgin olive oil
60 ml/¼ cup whole milk
1 egg, beaten
olive oil, for frying

TO SERVE

1 ripe avocado, peeled, pitted
   and sliced into thin half-moons
1 medium tomato, roughly
   chopped
50 ml/3½ tablespoons sour cream
salt and freshly ground black
   pepper

Combine the flour, baking powder, salt, pepper and chilli flakes/hot red pepper flakes in a large bowl and mix together. Add 165 g/5¾ oz. of the sweetcorn/corn (reserving the rest to serve) and mix again. Add the oil, milk and egg and stir together until well combined into a smooth batter with a dropping consistency. If the mixture is too thick, add a little more milk until it easily falls off a spoon. Set aside.

Put 1 tablespoon of olive oil in a frying pan/skillet over a medium heat. When the oil is hot, carefully drop dessertspoonfuls or small tablespoonfuls of the batter into the pan, at least 1-cm/½-inch apart, and flatten slightly with the back of the spoon. Cook for 3–4 minutes, then flip over and cook for 3–4 minutes on the other side until the pancakes are golden brown and cooked through. Remove to a warm plate and repeat for any remaining batter.

Alternatively, for a crispier finish, you can shallow-fry the pancakes in 0.5-cm/¼-inch layer of olive oil over a high heat for 2–3 minutes on each side, before removing and draining any excess oil on a paper towel.

For the topping, fry the remaining 100 g/3½ oz. sweetcorn/corn in a frying pan/skillet in a tablespoon of olive oil over a high heat until charred. Mix together the charred sweetcorn, avocado, tomato and salt and pepper to make a rough salsa. Serve the pancakes slightly warm, topped with a spoonful of sour cream, the salsa and extra black pepper.

TIP These mini pancakes are best served warm. If you are making them in advance, they can be reheated easily in a frying pan/skillet over a medium heat for 2–3 minutes.

strawberries & cream biskies

This biskie is our ultimate signature product. It is a fairly complicated recipe, but worthwhile as the result is this moreish and luscious treat.

DIFFICULTY ✎✎✎✎ | MAKES 12–15 | PREP TIME 2½ HOURS + CHILL TIME | BAKE TIME 10–15 MINUTES

VANILLA BISKIE DOUGH

85 g/¾ cup Vanilla Crumb (see page 13)

125 g/1⅛ sticks unsalted butter, softened

70 g/⅓ cup plus 1 teaspoon caster/granulated sugar

70 g/⅓ cup plus 1 teaspoon soft light brown sugar

1 teaspoon baking powder

1 teaspoon fine salt

2 eggs, at room temperature

50 g/¼ cup golden/light corn syrup

1 teaspoon vanilla bean paste

170 g/1¼ cups plain/all-purpose flour

TO ASSEMBLE

1 x batch Biskie Buttercream (see page 16)

1 teaspoon vanilla bean paste

30 g/1 oz. freeze-dried strawberry powder

250 g/9 oz. fresh strawberries

100 g/3½ oz. white chocolate, melted, to decorate

piping/pastry bag with a round plain 2-cm/¾-inch nozzle/tip

Prepare the vanilla crumb and set aside to cool.

Put the softened butter, both sugars, baking powder and salt in a mixing bowl. Beat with a hand-held electric whisk at medium speed (or use a stand mixer with the paddle attachment) until light and fluffy.

Scrape down the sides of the bowl and add the eggs and golden/light corn syrup. Beat for 10 minutes until the mixture is well combined – it should resemble thick yogurt.

Add the vanilla paste and vanilla crumb and sift in the flour. Beat in slowly at first, then at a medium speed for 1–2 minutes until well combined. Pop the mixture into a container, cover and refrigerate for about 1 hour until firm.

Preheat the oven to 180°C/fan 160°C (350°F) Gas 4. Scoop out 20 g/¾ oz. portions of the mixture and roll into balls. Space the balls out on two non-stick baking sheets, leaving a 4-cm/1½-inch gap either side as they will spread. Bake in the preheated oven for 10–15 minutes until golden at the edges. Transfer to a cooling rack to cool.

Prepare the biskie buttercream, then add the vanilla paste and freeze-dried strawberry powder and beat together. Reserve eight whole strawberries and thinly slice the rest.

To assemble the biskies, transfer the buttercream to the piping/pastry bag with a 2-cm/¾-inch plain nozzle/tip. Pipe a swirl on one biskie base, add a few slices of fresh strawberry, followed by another swirl of buttercream and a biskie top. Repeat for the remaining biskies.

To decorate, drizzle the melted white chocolate on top of the biskies and pipe a peak of buttercream on top of each. Halve the reserved strawberries and place one half on each. Serve immediately for best results. Or keep in the fridge for up to 3 days, they will soften but will still be delicious.

salted caramel brownies

When we swirled our award-winning salted caramel into this seriously good brownie mix, we knew we were on to something good. There are no rules on how gooey or firm your brownie should be – Mummy Lui likes hers cooked for a little longer, but this recipe makes the squidgy brownies that we prefer! Just cook for a few more or less minutes depending on your preference.

| DIFFICULTY | MAKES 9 | PREP TIME 30 MINUTES | BAKE TIME 20–25 MINUTES |

150 g/5½ oz. Salted Caramel Sauce (see page 22)
80 g/¾ stick unsalted butter
160 g/5⅔ oz. dark/bittersweet chocolate, broken into pieces
320 g/1½ cups plus 1 tablespoon caster/granulated sugar
6 eggs
80 g/generous ¾ cup cocoa powder
160 g/scant 1¼ cups plain/all-purpose flour or plain/all-purpose gluten-free flour
ice cream, to serve (optional)

23-cm/9-inch square baking pan, lined with greaseproof baking parchment

Prepare the salted caramel sauce and set aside.

Put the butter and chocolate pieces in a heatproof bowl and microwave in short bursts of 30 seconds, stirring gently each time, until melted and combined. Leave to cool until cold but still liquid.

Preheat the oven to 200°C/fan 180°C (400°F) Gas 6. Combine the sugar and eggs in a mixing bowl. Whisk together at a medium speed with a hand-held electric whisk (or use a stand mixer with the whisk attachment), until pale yellow, light and thick enough to hold the trail of a figure of eight.

Slowly add the cooled melted chocolate to the sugar and egg mixture, whisking to combine. Mix together the cocoa powder and flour, then slowly mix in until evenly combined.

Pour the brownie mix into the prepared pan and drizzle over the salted caramel sauce. Use a knife to gently swirl the caramel into the surface of the batter.

Bake in the preheated oven for 20–25 minutes until slightly risen with a light crust and still wobbly in the centre.

Leave to cool completely in the pan before cutting into even squares. Serve warm with ice cream for dessert or cold as a treat at any time of the day.

shortbread whirls with candied chilli pineapple

The smell of this candied pineapple cooking is seriously nostalgic for us. We created it for one of our first biskie flavours, and every time we cook it we are whisked back in time to our little home kitchen. The combination of buttery shortbread works so well with the fruity heat of the pineapple.

DIFFICULTY	MAKES 25–30	PREP TIME 35 MINUTES + CHILL TIME	BAKE TIME 8–10 MINUTES

CANDIED PINEAPPLE CENTRE
450 g/1 lb. canned pineapple in juice
freshly grated zest and squeezed juice of 1 lime
100 g/½ cup soft light brown sugar
½ teaspoon dried chilli flakes/ hot red pepper flakes

SHORTBREAD WHIRLS
250 g/2¼ sticks unsalted butter, softened
50 g/¼ cup caster/granulated sugar
50 g/generous ⅓ cup icing/ confectioners' sugar
1 teaspoon vanilla bean paste
275 g/2 cups plain/all-purpose flour
25 g/¼ cup cornflour/cornstarch

piping/pastry bag with a medium star-shaped nozzle/tip (approx. 1.5 cm/⅝-inch)
2 baking sheets, lined with greaseproof baking parchment

Drain the canned pineapple juice into a saucepan. Chop the pineapple into chunks and add to the saucepan. Add half the lime zest (reserving the rest) and all the juice, plus the brown sugar and dried chilli flakes/hot red pepper flakes and stir. Bring to the boil over a medium heat and let bubble for about 20 minutes until no liquid is left. Leave to cool.

Preheat the oven to 190°C/fan 170°C (375°F) Gas 5.

For the shortbread, put the softened butter, caster/ granulated sugar and icing/confectioners' sugar in a mixing bowl. Cream together at a medium speed with a hand-held electric whisk (or use a stand mixer with the paddle attachment) until light and fluffy. Mix in the vanilla paste. Sift in the flour and cornflour/cornstarch and mix until combined into a soft dough that should be easy to pipe.

Transfer the mixture to the piping/pastry bag with the star-shaped nozzle/tip and pipe 5-cm/2-inch swirls onto each prepared baking sheet, starting at the centre and working outwards. Leave a 3-cm/1¼-inch gap either side. (As there is enough mixture to make 25–30, you will need to bake these in batches.) Chill in the fridge for 15 minutes before baking.

Bake the first batch of shortbreads in the preheated oven for 8–10 minutes until turning golden at the edges. Remove from the oven and transfer to a cooling rack. Prepare, chill and then bake the remaining dough following the same steps.

When ready to serve, place a teaspoonful of the candied pineapple mixture onto the centre of each shortbread whirl. Sprinkle with the remaining lime zest and enjoy straight away!

blueberry & lemon cheesecake dream cake

This is one of our most popular cakes. It has quite a few components, but you can prep these the day before. You could also cheat a bit and buy good-quality blueberry jam and lemon curd, and use crushed digestive biscuits/graham crackers for the crumb if needed.

DIFFICULTY 🥄🥄🥄🥄🥄 **SERVES 10–12** | **PREP TIME 3 HOURS + CHILL TIME** | **BAKE TIME 25–30 MINUTES**

1 x batch 20-cm/8-inch Vanilla Cake Batter (see page 11)
150 ml/⅔ cup Lemon Soak (see page 19)
100 g/3½ oz. Blueberry Jam (see page 21)
100 g/3½ oz. Lemon Curd (see page 21)
1 x batch Cream Cheese Custard (see page 18)
100 g/3½ oz. Digestive Crumb (see page 13)
50 g/2 oz. fresh blueberries, to decorate
finely grated zest of 2 lemons, to decorate

BLUEBERRY AND LEMON BUTTERCREAM
½ x batch Light as a Feather Cake Buttercream (see page 16)
1 teaspoon freeze-dried blueberry powder
1 tablespoon finely grated lemon zest

3 x 20-cm/8-inch springform cake pans, bases lined with greaseproof baking parchment
cake board or cake stand
stepped spatula (optional)

Preheat the oven to 180°C/fan 160°C (350°F) Gas 4.

Prepare a batch of the 20-cm/8-inch vanilla cake batter and divide between the three pans. Bake in the preheated oven following the instructions on page 11. Cool in the pans for 5 minutes, then remove to a cooling rack to cool completely.

Meanwhile, prepare the remaining components and the light as a feather cake buttercream and set aside. In a separate small bowl, mix together the blueberry powder and lemon zest with 1 teaspoon water, then beat into the buttercream.

To assemble the cake, trim each sponge into a flat and even layer, each about 4-cm/1½-inches thick. Line the sides of one of the pans that you baked the sponges in with a double layer of greaseproof baking parchment, about 15 cm/6 inches high. Put the first sponge in the pan and drizzle over a third of the lemon soak. Take 150 g/5½ oz. of the blueberry and lemon buttercream and drop teaspoonfuls of it over the sponge in a random fashion. Spoon over half the blueberry jam in the same way, followed by half the lemon curd, then half of the custard. Finally, sprinkle over half of the digestive crumb. Add the next sponge layer and repeat the steps.

Add the last sponge layer and drizzle over the remaining lemon soak. Gently compress the top sponge down into the cake to make sure everything is well packed. Freeze the cake for 20 minutes or refrigerate for 40 minutes to set.

Carefully remove the pan and paper from the cake and transfer to a cake stand or board with a blob of buttercream underneath. Smooth the remaining buttercream over the top with a stepped spatula or flat knife. Decorate the cake with fresh blueberries and lemon zest.

chocolate & salted caramel heaven cake

We have made this cake since the inception of Cutter & Squidge; it is a showstopper!

DIFFICULTY 🥄🥄🥄🥄🥄 **SERVES 8–10** | **PREP TIME 2½ HOURS + CHILL TIME** | **BAKE TIME 30–35 MINUTES**

1 x batch 15-cm/6-inch Chocolate Cake Batter (see page 12)
1 x batch Light as a Feather Cake Buttercream (see page 16)
40 g/generous ⅓ cup cocoa powder
1 x batch Chocolate Syrup (see page 19)
125 g/4½ oz. Salted Caramel Sauce (see page 22)

CHOCOLATE GANACHE
350 ml/1½ cups double/heavy cream
200 g/7 oz. dark/bittersweet chocolate, broken into pieces

TO DECORATE
200 g/7 oz. dark/bittersweet chocolate, melted
fresh raspberries
1–2 sheets gold leaf

3 x 15-cm/6-inch springform cake pans, bases lined with greaseproof baking parchment
piping/pastry bag with a plain round 2-cm/¾-inch nozzle/tip
cake board or cake stand
cake scraper
baking sheet, lined with greaseproof baking parchment

Preheat the oven to 180°C/fan 160°C (350°F) Gas 4.

Divide the cake batter between the three pans and bake following the instructions on page 12. Leave to cool in the pan for 5 minutes, then remove to a cooling rack to cool fully.

For the ganache, put the cream into a saucepan over a medium heat until simmering. Turn off the heat, add the chocolate and stir until smooth. Cool to room temperature.

Prepare the buttercream, then add 175 g/6 oz. of the cooled chocolate ganache (reserve the rest for the drip) and the cocoa powder. Slowly mix until combined; do not overmix. Set aside. Prepare the chocolate syrup and the salted caramel.

To assemble, cut each sponge in half horizontally to give six even, thin layers. Line the sides of one of the pans that you baked the sponges in with a double layer of greaseproof baking parchment, about 15 cm/6 inches high. Put the first sponge in the pan and drizzle over 50 ml/3½ tablespoons of the chocolate syrup. Pipe a layer of buttercream and smooth over. Drizzle over 25 g/1 oz. of the salted caramel. Repeat the process for the remaining sponges but smooth only 1 tablespoon of buttercream over the top sponge. Freeze the cake for 20 minutes or refrigerate for 40 minutes to set.

Remove the pan and paper and transfer the cake to a stand or board with buttercream underneath. Pipe buttercream rings around the cake (see A, page 42). Use a cake scraper to smooth the buttercream around the cake (B), scraping any overspill onto the top. Refrigerate for 30 minutes.

Warm the reserved ganache in the microwave until just melted and cool to room temperature. Spoon half over the cake, using a spoon to make it drip over the edges (C).

Spread the melted chocolate over the prepared baking sheet. Freeze for 10 minutes, then break into shards. Push the shards into the cake. Decorate with raspberries and gold leaf.

matcha, raspberry & white chocolate chunk cookies

Cookies should be simple, fun and delicious, and these are exactly that! Matcha green tea is the best quality green tea you can buy and it is considered a superfood due to its antioxidant properties. You don't need much of this magic powder to impart a wonderful hint of flavour and a beautiful green colour to these chunky cookies.

DIFFICULTY | **MAKES 6** | **PREP TIME 15 MINUTES** | **BAKE TIME 14 MINUTES**

125 g/1⅛ sticks unsalted butter
225 g/1¾ cups plain/all-purpose flour
1 teaspoon fine salt
10 g/¼ oz. matcha powder
¾ teaspoon baking powder
90 g/½ cup minus 2 teaspoons caster/granulated sugar
90 g/½ cup minus 2 teaspoons soft light brown sugar
1 egg

TOPPINGS
60 g/2¼ oz. white chocolate bar (the thick kind)
60 g/2¼ oz. fresh raspberries, roughly torn in half

baking sheet, lined with greaseproof baking parchment

Melt the butter in a saucepan and leave it to cool completely.

Preheat the oven to 220°C/fan 200°C (425°F) Gas 7.

Sift the flour, salt, matcha powder and baking powder into a large mixing bowl. Add the caster/granulated sugar and soft light brown sugar and stir until evenly combined. Add the egg and the cooled melted butter and mix with a wooden spoon until the mixture comes together into a soft dough.

Divide the dough into six equal portions and roll into large balls (or 12 medium balls if you want to make smaller cookies). Space the balls of dough out on the prepared baking sheet (they will spread as they bake) and flatten them down a little with your fingertips so that you can fit the toppings on.

Break the white chocolate roughly into large chunks and dig three large chunks lightly into the surface of each large cookie. Gently push 2–3 fresh raspberries into the surface of each cookie. Bake in the preheated oven for 14 minutes.

These cookies are unbelievable when served warm and almost straight out of the oven, but transfer them to a cooling rack if you are serving them as afternoon treats with a cup of tea or coffee.

salted caramel cake truffles

These luxurious cake truffles are a great way to use up any leftover scraps of cake, but it is also worth baking a cake solely to make them. They will keep for up to 1 week in the fridge and make a great gift.

DIFFICULTY 🥄	MAKES 10–12	PREP TIME 45 MINUTES + CHILL TIME	BAKE TIME N/A

200 g/7 oz. leftover vanilla cake sponge (or ½ batch 15-cm/ 6-inch Vanilla Cake Batter, see page 11)

½ x batch Vanilla Crumb (see page 13)

100 g/3½ oz. Salted Caramel Sauce (see page 22)

100 g/3½ oz. white chocolate, melted

large tray or plate lined with greaseproof baking parchment

Prepare the vanilla cake batter (if needed) and bake in one pan for 20–25 minutes. Prepare the vanilla crumb and then the salted caramel sauce following the instructions in the basic recipes. Set all aside to cool.

Using your hands, finely crumble the cake sponge into a mixing bowl. Mix in the salted caramel with a wooden spoon to form a dough-like mixture. Roll the mixture into 10–12 balls (the size of ping pong balls), then place on the prepared tray or plate and refrigerate for 30 minutes until firm.

Dip each cake truffle into the melted white chocolate and turn to cover them completely, then roll in the vanilla crumb to coat. Pop back into the fridge for 10 minutes to set.

TIP You can easily substitute the vanilla sponge for chocolate to make delicious chocolate caramel cake truffles.

lychee & rose latte

Lychee is a classic oriental flavour, popular in the Far East in sweets, desserts and drinks and we LOVE it. The rose water in this recipe really brings out the delicate lychee flavour. We use our own lychee and peach white tea for this recipe (available in store or online), but you can use any fragrant white tea blend.

1 teaspoon loose lychee peach tea
  (or another fragrant white tea blend)
250 ml/1 cup plus 1 tablespoon boiling water
½ teaspoon beetroot/beet powder
½ teaspoon white sugar
½ teaspoon rose water
300 ml/1¼ cups whole milk, coconut milk
  or oat milk
food-safe rose petals and/or crushed freeze-
  dried raspberries, to decorate

SERVES 2

Brew the lychee peach tea (or other fragrant white tea blend) in the boiling water following the instructions on the packet and pour into your favourite mugs.

Divide the beetroot/beet powder, sugar and rose water between the mugs and stir until dissolved.

Put the milk into a small saucepan and warm through over a low heat, whisking until it steams and is frothy. Or use a milk frother if you have one. Pour the milk over the pink tea.

Decorate the drinks with food-safe rose petals and some crushed freeze-dried raspberries. Enjoy.

raspberry, lemon & mint iced green tea

We have created our own range of iced teas at the bakery, each with different qualities. This is known as our 'refresh' iced tea – a chilled green tea base with fresh fruit purée and zingy lemon and mint. It's perfect with afternoon tea on a hot summer's day or even served as a mocktail at a party.

150 g/5½ oz. fresh raspberries
50 g/¼ cup soft light brown sugar (optional)
2 green tea bags
1 litre/quart boiling water

TO SERVE
plenty of ice
5 small sprigs fresh mint
1 lemon, cut into slices

SERVES 5

Place 100 g/3½ oz. of the raspberries in a food processor (reserving the rest) and blend to a smooth purée. Sieve/strain the purée to remove any seeds. Taste the purée – if your raspberries are sour, then mix in the brown sugar. Set aside.

Put the green tea bags into the boiling water and leave to brew until the water is cold, then remove the tea bags.

To serve, place 20 g/¾ oz. of the raspberry purée in each glass. Add some ice, then top up with some of the cold green tea and stir. Alternatively, you could stir together all the raspberry purée and green tea in a large jug/pitcher over ice to serve.

Garnish each glass with a couple of the reserved raspberries, a small mint sprig and a slice of lemon.

FANTASY
afternoon tea

This section contains some of the most popular items from the afternoon teas served in our store. Themes include Hello Kitty's Secret Garden, Genie's Cave and The Potion Room.

'rose' courgette tartlets

These tartlets were served in our Genie's Cave afternoon tea. While they look delicate and pretty, they are actually easy to make and very tasty.

DIFFICULTY 🥄🥄🥄 | **MAKES 8–10** | **PREP TIME 1 HOUR + CHILL TIME** | **BAKE TIME 28 MINUTES**

½ batch Sweet Shortcrust Pastry (see page 14) minus the sugar
plain/all-purpose flour, for dusting
1 egg, beaten with 1 tablespoon of water, for brushing

FILLING
1 egg
125 ml/½ generous cup double/heavy cream
25 ml/1½ tablespoons whole milk
1 shallot or small white onion, finely chopped
50 g/1¾ oz. finely grated Parmesan cheese
¼ teaspoon fine salt
½ teaspoon freshly ground black pepper
1 good pinch ground nutmeg
3 courgettes/zucchini

10-cm/4-inch plain or fluted round cookie cutter or a glass just bigger than your pans
8–10 tartlet pans approx. 7.5-cm/3-inches in diameter, or a muffin pan

Prepare the shortcrust pastry, leaving out the sugar. Remove it from the fridge 10 minutes before using so that it is soft enough to roll out. Divide the pastry roughly in half and roll out one half on a lightly floured surface until thin but not transparent. Stamp out 5 circles using the round cutter or glass. Gently press each pastry circle into each tart mould using the back of a small spoon to help. The edge of the pastry should rise above the edge of the mould a little. Prick the bottom and sides of the pastry a few times with a fork. Bring the pastry scraps together into a ball with the other half of the pastry and repeat the steps to make 3-5 more cases. Refrigerate the pastry cases for at least 10 minutes to firm up.

Preheat the oven to 200°C/fan 180°C (400°F) Gas 6.

Brush the tart cases with the beaten egg, then bake in the preheated oven for 12 minutes until the pastry is cooked but pale. Remove and leave to cool slightly, but keep the oven on.

Meanwhile, in a jug/pitcher, whisk together the egg, cream, milk, shallot or onion, Parmesan, salt, pepper and nutmeg. Pour into each tart case to fill about two-thirds of the way up. Top and tail each courgette/zucchini, then use a vegetable peeler to shave them into fine long ribbons. Cut each ribbon in half lengthways so that each ribbon has the green skin on one edge. Place 8 half-ribbons on top of each other and gently roll into a spiral. Place inside a pastry case with the green edges facing upwards; it might open up slightly but this is fine. Repeat for the remaining courgette/zucchini and tart cases. Bake in the hot oven for 16 minutes until lightly golden brown. These are delicious served warm or cold.

feta & red pepper pinwheel scones

These were a very popular bake from our Genie's Cave afternoon tea,
our customers loved having a savoury twist to a traditional sweet scone.

DIFFICULTY 🥄🥄🥄	MAKES 12	PREP TIME 40 MINUTES	BAKE TIME 20 MINUTES

SCONES
210 g/1½ cups plain/all-purpose
   flour, plus extra for dusting
   the work surface
2 teaspoons baking powder
pinch of fine salt
35 g/1¼ oz. cold butter, diced
130 ml/generous ½ cup lukewarm
   whole milk

FILLING
50 g/1¾ oz. soft cheese with
   garlic and herbs, such as Boursin
½ teaspoon ras el hanout
1 red (bell) pepper, deseeded
   and finely diced
1 tablespoon finely chopped
   fresh parsley
½ teaspoon fine salt
½ teaspoon freshly ground
   black pepper
1 tablespoon vegetable oil
100 g/3½ oz. feta cheese,
   crumbled

*2 baking sheets, lined with
greaseproof baking parchment*

Preheat the oven to 220°C/fan 200°C (425°F) Gas 7.

Combine the flour, baking powder and salt in a mixing bowl. Add the butter and rub together with your fingertips to form a fine breadcrumb texture. Slowly mix in the lukewarm milk to bring the mixture together into a soft, sticky dough.

Heavily flour the work surface and your rolling pin. Form the dough roughly into a rectangle, then roll out to a large rectangle, about 15 x 40 cm/6 x 16 inches and 1-cm/½-inch thick. Cut a 50 cm/20 inch long piece of greaseproof baking parchment and carefully slide the dough onto it. Place it landscape in front of you, so one of the long edges is nearest you. Roughly spread the garlic and herb soft cheese all over the dough, then sprinkle the ras el hanout over the top.

In a separate small bowl, mix together the red (bell) pepper, parsley, salt, pepper and oil. Spread evenly over the dough but this time leaving a 1-cm/½-inch gap around the edge. Evenly crumble the feta over the top and gently press all the topping into the dough. You now need to roll the dough up like a Swiss roll/jelly roll, so take the long edge furthest away from you and roll it towards you tightly, using the baking parchment to help you form and squeeze the roll. The tighter your roll, the less likely your scones are to fall apart.

Use a sharp knife to trim and discard the untidy ends, then cut the roll into 3-cm/1¼-inch thick slices. Space the slices of dough out on the prepared baking sheets. Bake in the preheated oven for 20 minutes until lightly golden brown on the top. These are especially lovely served warm, so if needed warm through in the oven again before serving.

chocolate custard lollibag cakes

These were part of the sweet selection in our Genie's Cave afternoon tea, where they were adorned with flecks of real 24-carat gold leaf on the top! Cutting out the layers of sponge and assembling takes a little patience, but they look so cute and the ratio of cake to filling is perfect.

DIFFICULTY	**MAKES 12**	**PREP TIME 1½ HOURS + CHILL TIME**	**BAKE TIME 25–30 MINUTES**

1 x batch Chocolate Custard
(see page 18)
1 x 20-cm/8-inch Chocolate
Cake Batter (see page 12)
1 x batch Chocolate Syrup
(see page 19)

TO DECORATE
100 g/3½ oz. chocolate flakes
1 square gold leaf (optional)

*3 x rectangular Swiss roll/roulade
pans, around 20 x 18-cm/
8 x 7-inches, bases lined with
greaseproof baking parchment
stepped spatula
5-cm/2-inch plain round cookie
cutter
piping/pastry bag with a star-shaped
nozzle/tip*

First, prepare the chocolate custard and leave to chill for 1 hour before using.

Preheat the oven to 180°C/fan 160°C (350°F) Gas 4.

Prepare a batch of the 20-cm/8-inch chocolate cake batter and divide between the three rectangular cake pans, smoothing over the tops to level with a stepped spatula. Bake in the preheated oven following the instructions on page 12. Leave to cool in the pans for 5 minutes, then remove the cakes to a cooling rack to cool completely.

Prepare the chocolate syrup and set aside.

Trim the sponges so they are even, then stamp out 36 rounds of cake using the 5-cm/2-inch round cutter.

To assemble the cakes, put the chilled chocolate custard into the piping/pastry bag with a star-shaped nozzle/tip.

Brush a circle of sponge with a little warm chocolate syrup to moisten, then pipe on a peak of set chocolate custard. Add the next sponge layer and repeat the same steps for the syrup and custard. Sandwich the final round of sponge on top, brush with syrup and pipe a small peak of custard on top to crown the cake. Repeat for the remaining sponge pieces, you should have 12 individual cakes.

Decorate the cakes with a sprinkling of crumbled chocolate flakes and a little gold leaf, if you like.

TIP You can use these sponge offcuts to make some amazing cake truffles (see page 47).

apple pie mousse with shortbread bows

All of you who know Hello Kitty will know that apple pie is her favourite food. We created this for our Hello Kitty Secret Garden afternoon tea. The shortbread bows are cute as a button and delicious dipped into the mousse!

DIFFICULTY ✎✎✎	MAKES 6	PREP TIME 1 HOUR + CHILL TIME	BAKE TIME 10–15 MINUTES

1 x batch Apple Jam (see page 21)
1 tart green eating apple, such as Granny Smith, peeled, cored and finely chopped

APPLE PIE MOUSSE
150 g/5½ oz. white chocolate, broken into pieces
4 UK large/US extra-large egg whites
1 tablespoon caster/granulated sugar
200 ml/scant 1 cup double/ heavy cream
1 teaspoon ground cinnamon, plus extra to decorate

SHORTBREAD BOWS
200 g/1¾ sticks unsalted butter, softened
90 g/scant ½ cup caster/ granulated sugar, plus extra for dusting
290 g/2 cups plus 3 tablespoons plain/all-purpose flour

6 small serving glasses or jars
cookie cutter in a bow shape or fantasy shape of your choice
baking sheet, lined with greaseproof baking parchment

Make the apple jam and leave to cool. Mix the chopped apple into the jam, divide between your serving glasses and set aside.

To make the mousse, melt the white chocolate in a heatproof bowl set over a pan of barely simmering water, then remove from the heat and leave until cool but still runny.

Put the egg whites into a separate mixing bowl and use a hand-held electric whisk to whisk them to stiff peaks. Add the sugar and briefly whisk again to incorporate. Set aside.

In a another bowl, whip the cream to soft peaks, then fold in the melted white chocolate and the cinnamon. Add a spoonful of the stiff egg whites to the cream mixture and stir well. Fold in the remaining egg whites, working quickly but taking care not to knock out too much air. Divide the mousse between the glasses or jars on top of the jam. Cover with clingfilm/plastic wrap and refrigerate for 1 hour until set.

Meanwhile, make the shortbreads. Put the butter and sugar into a mixing bowl and cream together using a hand-held electric whisk (or use a stand mixer with the paddle attachment) until light and fluffy. Sift in the flour and mix with a wooden spoon to bring together into a dough. Roll out the dough between two sheets of greaseproof baking parchment to roughly 1-cm/½-inch thick. Transfer the dough, between the paper, to the fridge for 10–15 minutes to firm up.

Preheat the oven to 190°C/fan 170°C (375°F) Gas 5.

Use the bow-shaped cutter or the cutter of your choice to cut out cookies and place on the prepared baking sheet. Dust with caster/granulated sugar, then bake in the preheated oven for 10–15 minutes or until pale golden brown. Leave to cool.

To serve, place a cookie in each glass or jar of mousse and decorate with an extra sprinkle of cinnamon.

magic carpet cookies

These light, crisp and buttery cookies are delicious with a cup of tea or a latte. They are really easy to make, so are perfect for baking with kids. You can omit the stamp or get creative and use any design you like!

DIFFICULTY ✎	MAKES 12–15	PREP TIME 30 MINUTES + CHILL TIME	BAKE TIME 15–20 MINUTES

250 g/2¼ sticks unsalted butter, softened
50 g/¼ cup caster/granulated sugar
50 g/generous ⅓ cup icing/confectioners' sugar
1 teaspoon vanilla bean paste
225 g/1¾ cups plain/all-purpose flour
25 g/¼ cup cornflour/cornstarch
50 g/½ cup cocoa powder, for stamping

5 x 7.5-cm/3 x 2-inch rectangular cookie cutter
2 baking sheets, lined with greaseproof baking parchment
patterned stamp of your choice

Preheat the oven to 180°C/fan 160°C (350°F) Gas 4.

Put the butter, caster/granulated sugar and icing/confectioners' sugar in a mixing bowl. Cream together at a medium speed with a hand-held electric whisk (or use a stand mixer with the paddle attachment) until light and fluffy.

Add the vanilla bean paste and mix in. Sift in the plain/all-purpose flour and cornflour/cornstarch and mix with a wooden spoon until the mixture comes together into a dough.

Roll out the dough between two sheets of greaseproof baking parchment until it is about 5-mm/¼-inch thick. Carefully transfer the dough, still between the parchment, to the fridge and leave for 10–15 minutes to firm up.

Use your cookie cutter to cut out rectangles and space out on the prepared baking sheets.

Tip the cocoa powder onto a plate in a thin layer and dip your stamp into it. Stamp each cookie with your pattern, loading up with a little more cocoa powder each time. We have used a stamp with diamond shapes to make it look like a magic carpet. Chill the cookies for 30 minutes in the fridge.

Bake in the preheated oven for 15–20 minutes until they are cooked with only a very light golden edge. Leave to cool and then they are ready for your afternoon tea table!

ombre rainbow layer cake

Your friends and family won't believe that this showstopper
is made without a single bottle of food colouring in sight.

DIFFICULTY 🥄🥄🥄🥄🥄   **SERVES 8–10**   **PREP TIME 3 HOURS +
CHILL TIME**   **BAKE TIME 20–25 MINUTES**

1 x batch 15-cm/6-inch Vanilla
   Cake Batter (see page 11)
1 x batch Vanilla Syrup
   (see page 19)
20 g/¾ oz. all-natural coloured
   sprinkles

RAINBOW BUTTERCREAM
1 x batch Light as a Feather
   Buttercream (see page 16)
2 g ground turmeric, mixed into
   a paste with 1 teaspoon water
2 g green spirulina, mixed into
   a paste with 1 teaspoon water
2 g blue spirulina, mixed into
   a paste with 1 teaspoon water
2 g blueberry powder, mixed into
   a paste with 1 teaspoon water
2 g beetroot/beet powder, mixed
   into a paste with 1 teaspoon
   water

*3 x 15-cm/6-inch springform cake
   pans, greased and lined with
   greaseproof baking parchment
5 x disposable piping/pastry bags
cake board or cake stand
cake scraper*

Preheat the oven to 180°C/fan 160°C (350°F) Gas 4.

Prepare a batch of the 15-cm/6-inch vanilla cake batter
and divide between the three cake pans. Bake in the
preheated oven following the instructions on page 11.

When cool, trim the sponges to flat, even layers. Cut each
sponge in half horizontally so that you have six thin layers.

Prepare the buttercream. Stir the yellow paste into
200 g/7 oz. of the buttercream and the rest of the coloured
pastes each into 175 g/6 oz. of the buttercream separately.

Prepare the vanilla syrup and set aside.

Line the sides of one of the pans that you baked the
sponges in with a double layer of greaseproof baking
parchment, about 15 cm/6 inches high. Put the first sponge in
the pan and drizzle over 50 ml/3½ tablespoons of warm vanilla
syrup. Transfer the green buttercream to piping/pastry bag
and cut a small hole in the end (see A, page 64). Pipe on about
100 g/3½ oz. of the buttercream and smooth over. Add the
next sponge and push down gently. Repeat the steps with the
syrup, coloured buttercream and sponges, adding blue, purple,
pink and yellow. Add the sixth layer and syrup. Freeze the
cake for 20 minutes or refrigerate for 40 minutes to set.

Remove the pan and paper and transfer the cake to a
board or cake stand with a blob of buttercream underneath.
Pipe two rings of green buttercream around the bottom of the
cake, about 2.5-cm/1-inch high (B). Follow this with two rings
of the blue, purple, pink and finally the yellow. Place the
remaining yellow buttercream on top and smooth over with a
spatula (C). Use a scraper to smooth the buttercream around
the cake (D), cleaning the scraper as you go. Scrape any
overspill onto the top of the cake. To finish, pipe eight rainbow
peaks around the top edge and add all-natural sprinkles.

pearl biskies

Our pearl biskies are a best seller and we have created them in many different flavours; this particular version is white chocolate and tangy raspberry.

DIFFICULTY 🥄🥄🥄🥄 | **MAKES 12–15** | **PREP TIME 2½ HOURS + CHILL TIME** | **BAKE TIME 10–15 MINUTES**

VANILLA BISKIE DOUGH

85 g/¾ cup Vanilla Crumb (see page 13)

125 g/1⅛ sticks unsalted butter, softened

70 g/⅓ cup plus 1 teaspoon caster/granulated sugar

70 g/⅓ cup plus 1 teaspoon soft light brown sugar

1 teaspoon baking powder

1 teaspoon fine salt

2 eggs, at room temperature

50 g/¼ cup golden/corn syrup

1 teaspoon vanilla bean paste

170 g/1¼ cups plain/all-purpose flour

TO ASSEMBLE

20 g/¾ oz. freeze-dried raspberry powder

1 x batch Biskie Buttercream (see page 16)

150 g/5½ oz. white chocolate

20 g/¾ oz. freeze-dried raspberry pieces

¼ teaspoon ground turmeric

100 g/3½ oz. natural fondant icing

1 teaspoon all-natural sprinkles

12–15 white chocolate truffles

piping/pastry bag with a plain round 2 cm/¾-inch nozzle/tip

small star-shaped cookie cutter

Prepare the vanilla crumb and set aside to cool.

Put the softened butter, both sugars, baking powder and salt in a bowl a mixing bowl. Beat together at a high speed with a hand-held electric whisk (or use a stand mixer with the paddle attachment) until light and fluffy.

Scrape down the sides of the bowl and add the eggs and golden/light corn syrup. Beat for 10 minutes at a medium speed until well combined – it should resemble thick yogurt.

Add the vanilla bean paste and vanilla crumb and sift in the flour. Beat for 1–2 minutes to combine. Pop the mixture into a container, cover and refrigerate for about 1 hour until firm.

Preheat the oven to 180°C/fan 160°C (350°F) Gas 4.

Scoop out 20 g/¾ oz. portions of the mix. Roll into balls and space out over two non-stick baking sheets, with 4-cm/1½-inch gaps each side. Bake in the preheated oven for 10–15 minutes until the edges are golden. Cool.

Meanwhile, prepare the buttercream. Mix the raspberry powder with 1 tablespoon of water and stir into the buttercream. Transfer to the piping/pastry bag.

Melt the white chocolate and roll the biskie edges in, then roll them in the freeze-dried raspberry pieces. Leave to dry.

Add the turmeric to the fondant paste and knead in. Roll the fondant icing out on a surface sprinkled with icing/confectioners' sugar to 5-mm/¼-inch thick. Use the star cutter to cut out 12–15 starfish decorations. Push a sprinkle into the centre of each star, using a little water to help it stick.

To assemble the biskies, turn half flat-side up, pipe on a swirl of buttercream and place a white chocolate truffle in the centre, with a fondant starfish on the side. Place another half on top, flat-side down, touching at one edge so they look like open oyster shells! Refrigerate for 30 minutes before serving.

vegan cauldron cupcakes

These heavenly little chocolate fudge cakes are so simple to make and you can't even tell that they are vegan. They were part of our vegan Potion Room afternoon tea selection and our customers loved them.

DIFFICULTY ✎✎✎ | **MAKES 24** | **PREP TIME 45 MINUTES** + **CHILL TIME** | **BAKE TIME 25-30 MINUTES**

VEGAN CHOCOLATE SPONGE
80 ml/scant ⅓ cup vegetable oil
1 tablespoon apple cider vinegar
2 teaspoons vanilla bean paste
90 g/⅔ cup plain/all-purpose flour
200 g/1 cup caster/granulated sugar
70 g/scant ¾ cup good-quality cocoa powder
1 teaspoon baking powder
½ teaspoon bicarbonate of soda/ baking soda
1 teaspoon fine salt

CHOCOLATE HANDLES
100 g/3½ oz. vegan dark/ bittersweet chocolate

WHIPPED CHOCOLATE FROSTING
200 g/7 oz. vegan dark/ bittersweet chocolate
90 g/3¼ oz. coconut oil
90 ml/⅓ cup vegetable oil
90 g/⅔ cup icing/ confectioners' sugar

24-hole mini muffin pan lined with 24 mini muffin cases
piping/pastry bag with a small plain nozzle/tip and one with a large 10-point star nozzle/tip
2 baking sheets, lined with greaseproof baking parchment

Preheat the oven to 190°C/fan 170°C (375°F) Gas 5.

Put all the wet ingredients for the sponge with 250 ml/ 1 cup plus 1 tablespoon water in a mixing bowl. Sift all the dry ingredients into a separate bowl and mix together. Slowly add the dry ingredients to the wet ingredients, mixing with a hand-held electric whisk at a medium speed (or use a stand mixer with the paddle attachment) until combined.

Spoon the mixture into the mini muffin cases, about 25 g/1 oz. per cake, and bake in the preheated oven for 20–25 minutes until risen and set. Leave to cool completely.

To make the handles, melt the chocolate in a heatproof bowl set over a pan of barely simmering water. Transfer the chocolate to the piping/pastry bag with a small plain nozzle/tip and pipe 24 three-quarter circle shapes onto the prepared baking sheets – they need to be nice and thick, so go over them a few times. Refrigerate for 20 minutes until set.

To make the frosting, put the chocolate and coconut oil in a heatproof bowl and melt in the microwave in short bursts, checking and stirring often. Add the vegetable oil and sift in the icing/confectioners' sugar. Mix together well. Cool a little, then refrigerate for 30 minutes until thickened.

Place the chilled frosting in a mixing bowl or the bowl of a stand mixer and whip using a hand-held electric whisk or the whisk attachment until mousse-like in texture. (If the frosting is too hard, melt half in the microwave until liquid, then pour back over the rest and whip.) Transfer the frosting to the piping/pastry bag with the large 10-point star nozzle/tip. Pipe a large star on top of each cupcake, then place the chocolate handles into the frosting.

pink thumbprint cookies

These pink cookie bites flavoured with vanilla and homemade raspberry jam just melt in the mouth. They are so moreish you will find it hard to keep up with demand! Luckily they are super easy to make and a great one for kids to help out with. As beetroot/beet powder is used instead of artificial food colouring, you will need to keep an eye on them as they bake so they don't turn too brown.

DIFFICULTY | **MAKES 20–25** | **PREP TIME 45 MINUTES** | **BAKE TIME 10–12 MINUTES**

125 g/1⅛ sticks unsalted butter, softened
25 g/2 tablespoons caster/granulated sugar
25 g/2¾ tablespoons icing/confectioners' sugar
1 teaspoon vanilla bean paste
135 g/1 cup plain/all-purpose flour
15 g/2½ tablespoons cornflour/cornstarch
10 g/2 teaspoons beetroot/beet powder
100 g/½ cup caster/granulated sugar, for coating
100 g/3½ oz. Raspberry Jam (see page 21)

2 baking sheets, lined with greaseproof baking parchment

Preheat the oven to 190°C/fan 170°C (375°F) Gas 5.

Put the softened butter, caster/granulated sugar and icing/confectioners' sugar in a mixing bowl. Cream together at a medium speed with a hand-held electric whisk (or use a stand mixer with the paddle attachment) until light and fluffy.

Add the vanilla bean paste and mix in. Sift in the plain/all-purpose flour, cornflour/cornstarch and beetroot/beet powder together and mix again to combine into a soft dough.

Scoop out 15 g/½ oz. portions of dough and roll into balls. Roll the balls in a plate of caster/granulated sugar to evenly coat, then transfer to the prepared baking sheets, leaving a 5-cm/2-inch gap between each cookie. Use your thumb to make a firm but shallow indentation on each cookie. Place ½ teaspoonful of raspberry jam in the indent on each cookie.

Bake in the preheated oven for 10–12 minutes until the cookies are very light brown at the edges.

Remove from the oven and leave to cool on a cooling rack before serving.

unicorn sours

This is one for the adults only! Also created for our Potion Room afternoon tea, the natural chemical reaction between the citrus alcohol base and the blue pea tea is beautiful to look at. Topped with popping candy, this is a fun drink that will play on all your senses.

120 ml/½ cup vodka
120 ml/½ cup limoncello
75 ml/⅓ cup freshly squeezed lemon juice
10 teaspoons Vanilla Syrup (see page 19)

TO SERVE
plenty of ice
3 blue pea tea bag, brewed in 1 litre/quart boiling water, cooled
popping candy and edible flowers, to garnish

5 serving glasses

SERVES 5

Stir together the vodka, limoncello, lemon juice and vanilla syrup in a jug/pitcher.

Fill each serving glass with ice, then add 50 ml/3½ tablespoons of the vodka mixture to each glass. Sprinkle each drink with popping candy and garnish with edible flowers

To serve, remove the tea bag and then top up each glass with cold blue pea tea. Watch the colours change!

galaxy juice

We created this eye-catching non-alcoholic drink to be served alongside our Potion Room afternoon tea. It is simple to make, but the natural, vibrant hues of the different teas and juice make for a magical effect.

plenty of crushed ice or big cubes of ice
150 ml/⅔ cup store-bought passion fruit juice
1 berry tea bag, brewed in 100 ml/⅓ cup plus 1 tablespoon boiling water, cooled
1 blue pea tea bag, brewed in 100 ml/⅓ cup plus 1 tablespoon boiling water, cooled

2 tall serving glasses and paper straws

SERVES 2

Fill your two serving glasses almost to the top with ice (this will help with separation of the liquids). Add the passion fruit juice to each glass. Remove the tea bags from both teas and then slowly pour half the cold berry tea into each glass.

Slowly top up each glass with half the cold blue pea tea and serve with paper straws.

You can also make this drink in one large jug/pitcher or glass bottle to show off the colours before serving.

CLASSIC BRITISH
afternoon tea

We are proud of being British and take so much inspiration from traditional great British food. In this section, you will find classic British flavours, but with a Cutter & Squidge twist!

filled mini yorkshire puddings

There is nothing more classically British than a Yorkshire pud! These are bite-sized but pack a punch from the creamed horseradish and the peppery watercress. For a vegetarian alternative, you could substitute the toppings for chopped roasted (bell) peppers with a sprinkle of feta.

DIFFICULTY   **MAKES 12**   **PREP TIME 25 MINUTES**   **BAKE TIME 15 MINUTES**

vegetable oil, for oiling the pan
40 g/generous ¼ cup plain/
   all-purpose flour
½ teaspoon fine salt
½ teaspoon freshly ground black
   pepper, plus extra to serve
1 egg, beaten
50 ml/3½ tablespoons whole milk

TO SERVE
4 tablespoons crème fraîche
2 tablespoons creamed
   horseradish (or to taste)
2–3 large slices leftover roast beef
   (or from a deli)
small handful watercress sprigs

12-hole non-stick mini muffin pan

Preheat the oven to 220°C/fan 200°C (425°F) Gas 7.

Pour ½ teaspoon of vegetable oil into each of the 12 holes in the muffin pan and place in the hot oven for 5 minutes to heat up.

Sift the flour, salt and pepper into a bowl and stir together. Make a well in the centre and crack the egg into the well. Beat in the egg with a whisk, gradually incorporating the flour until smooth. Gradually add the milk and whisk in until the batter has no lumps and all the milk has been incorporated.

Carefully retrieve the muffin pan with the hot oil from the oven and divide the batter between each hole, approx. 3 teaspoons into each. Cook in the preheated oven for 15 minutes until the Yorkshire puddings have risen well and are golden. Transfer to a cooling rack to cool.

For the horseradish cream, mix the crème fraîche and creamed horseradish together, adding more horseradish to suit your taste. Set aside.

Cut the roast beef into 12 pieces.

To assemble, make a little cut in the top of each Yorkshire pudding and tuck a slice of beef in vertically. Spoon ½-1 teaspoon of the horseradish cream over the top. Garnish each Yorkshire with a watercress sprig and finish with a little freshly ground black pepper. Serve immediately.

creamy leek & potato pies

These little pies are the edible equivalent of a comforting hug! If you don't have time to make your own pastry, then just use store-bought instead.

DIFFICULTY 🥄🥄🥄   MAKES 8   PREP TIME 1 HOUR + CHILL TIME   BAKE TIME 25 MINUTES

1 x batch Rough Puff Pastry
(see page 15)
1 tablespoon vegetable oil
1 small baking potato
(e.g. Maris Piper), peeled
and cut into small cubes
1 leek (roughly 10-cm/4-inches),
thinly sliced into half-moons
1 pinch fine salt
1 pinch freshly ground black
pepper
1 tablespoon plain/all-purpose
flour, plus extra for dusting
the work surface
175 ml/¾ cup whole milk
75 g/2¾ oz. grated mature/sharp
Cheddar cheese
1 egg beaten with 1 tablespoon
water, for brushing

*10-cm/4-inch plain round cookie
cutter*
*baking sheet, lined with greaseproof
baking parchment*

Prepare the rough puff pastry and chill in the fridge.

Put the vegetable oil into a saucepan over a medium heat. Add the potato, leek, salt and black pepper and cook, stirring regularly, for 20 minutes until the potato is nearly cooked.

Meanwhile, take your rough puff pastry out of the fridge and let it warm up a little so you can roll it easily. Set aside.

Add the flour to the potato in the pan and mix well. Add the milk in three lots, mixing in well each time. Add the grated cheese and mix well again. Cook for about 12 minutes until the mixture thickens so much that it holds together; if it's too runny the pies will leak. Turn off the heat and set aside.

Cut the pastry roughly in half. Roll one half out on a lightly floured surface to a thickness of about 0.5-cm/¼-inch.

Stamp out four circles from the pastry with the round cutter, reserving the scraps. Place approx. 1 tablespoonful of filling into the middle of a pastry circle. Lightly wet the edge of one half of the pastry circle (to help it stick) and fold over the opposite edge to enclose the filling and make a half-moon shape. Carefully seal the edge by pressing the tips of a fork along the join to ensure the filling does not leak out during baking. Repeat for the remaining pastry circles.

Gently knead the pastry scraps together with the remaining pastry half, roll out and repeat the above steps until all eight are made. Place on the prepared baking sheet and brush the pies with the beaten egg mixture wash. Chill in the fridge for 10 minutes.

Preheat the oven to 200°C/fan 180°C (400°F) Gas 6.

Bake the pies in the preheated oven for 25 minutes or until golden brown. These are delicious served warm.

pork, stuffing & cranberry sausage rolls

This recipe really pushes a traditional sausage roll to the next level.
The stuffing keeps the filling moist and the chopped cranberries
give a pleasant tart, fruity bite.

DIFFICULTY	SERVES 8-10	PREP TIME 30 MINUTES + CHILL TIME	BAKE TIME 50 MINUTES

1 x batch Rough Puff Pastry
   (see page 15)
75 g/2¾ oz. ready-made dried
   sage and onion stuffing mix
knob/pat of butter for the stuffing
   (optional)
275 g/9¾ oz. pork sausage meat
   (or approx. 5 pork sausages
   removed from their casings)
50 g/1¾ oz dried cranberries,
   roughly chopped
plain/all-purpose flour, for dusting
   the work surface
1 egg, beaten with 1 tablespoon
   water, for brushing

baking sheet, lined with greaseproof
   baking parchment

Prepare the rough puff pastry and chill in the fridge. Remove from the fridge 10 minutes before using to let it warm up a little so you can roll it easily. Set aside.

Make up the stuffing mix in a large bowl as per the packet instructions but using a quarter (25%) less water and butter (you can omit the butter entirely if you wish). Leave to cool.

Add the sausage meat and dried cranberries to the cooled stuffing and mix together well.

Roll the pastry out on a lightly floured work surface to a large rectangle about 45 x 30-cm/18 x 12-inches. Cut the pastry in half lengthways and place one half on the prepared baking sheet. Place the meat filling in a long sausage shape lengthways down the centre of the pastry. Brush the beaten egg mixture around the edges of the pastry (to help it stick). Place the other pastry half neatly on top of the sausage meat to enclose. Carefully seal the edges by pressing the pastry together and crimping the edges with your fingers, or make indents with the prongs of a fork. Brush the pastry with the beaten egg mixture for a shiny brown finish, then chill in the fridge for 10 minutes to firm up.

Preheat the oven to 200°C/fan 180°C (400°F) Gas 6.

Bake the sausage roll in the preheated oven for 50 minutes until lightly golden brown. Cut into slices to serve. Delicious served warm or cold with your afternoon tea.

lemon treacle tarts

The proof is all in the eating with these tarts! Don't worry if your pastry cases aren't perfectly shaped and trimmed, or if your fresh breadcrumbs seem too big (they magically melt away during baking!). The umptious, zesty, treacly filling in these tarts is so good that no one will be looking at them for very long!

DIFFICULTY 🥄🥄🥄	MAKES 8–10	PREP TIME 40 MINUTES + CHILL TIME	BAKE TIME 15 MINUTES

½ x batch Sweet Shortcrust Pastry (see page 14)

plain/all-purpose flour, for dusting the work surface

60 g/1 generous cup fresh white breadcrumbs (approx. 1½ slices of bread finely chopped)

300 g/scant 1 cup golden/light corn syrup

finely grated zest of 1 lemon and freshly squeezed juice of ½ icing/confectioners' sugar, for dusting

edible flowers, to decorate

9-cm/3½-inch round cookie cutter of a glass just bigger than your tartlet pans

8–10 non-stick tartlet pans, 7.5-cm/3-inches in diameter

Make a batch of sweet shortcrust pastry and chill in the fridge. Remove the pastry from the fridge 10 minutes before you want to use it, so that it is soft enough to roll out.

Roll out the pastry on a lightly floured surface to approx. 3-mm/⅛-inch thick and stamp out 8–10 rounds with the cookie cutter or glass.

Press the pastry into the tart pans using the back of a spoon to help you make sure they are evenly thin and leaving a little lip of pastry to allow for the pastry shrinking a little as it bakes. Prick the tart cases all over with a fork, then chill in the fridge for 15 minutes to let the pastry firm up.

Preheat the oven to 200°C/fan 180°C (400°F) Gas 6.

Bake the tart cases in the preheated oven for 10 minutes. Remove from the oven, but leave the oven on. Let the tart cases cool a little while you prepare the filling.

Meanwhile, for the filling, put the fresh white breadcrumbs, golden/light corn syrup and lemon zest and juice in a bowl. Mix together until well combined. Spoon the mixture into the tart cases, filling all the way to the top, but leaving a slight gap for the mixture to bubble up. Bake again in the hot oven for 20–25 minutes until the filling is set and the pastry is golden.

Leave the tarts to cool in the pans before turning out and serving dusted with icing/confectioners' sugar and each decorated with an edible flower.

rock cake scones

When you don't have time to roll out dough and carefully cut out scones, making sure you don't twist them and ruin their rise – turn to THIS recipe! You can knock out killer rock cake scones in minutes and you won't need to worry about them not rising. Foolproof scones can be found right here!

DIFFICULTY | **MAKES 15–20** | **PREP TIME 10 MINUTES** | **BAKE TIME 20 MINUTES**

420 g/scant 3¼ cups plain/
   all-purpose flour
4½ teaspoons baking powder
¼ teaspoon fine salt
140 g/¾ cup minus 2 teaspoons
   caster/granulated sugar
70 g/⅔ stick cold unsalted
   butter, diced
260 ml/1 cup plus 1½ tablespoons
   whole milk
1 egg, beaten
30 g/scant ¼ cup soft dark
   brown sugar, for the topping
homemade jam (see page 21)
   and clotted cream, to serve

ice-cream scoop
2 baking sheets, lined with
   greaseproof baking parchment

Preheat the oven to 220°C/fan 200°C (425°F) Gas 7.

Combine the flour, baking powder, salt and caster/granulated sugar in a bowl. Add the cold diced butter and rub together with your fingertips until the mixture is the texture of fine breadcrumbs.

Warm the milk very slightly in the microwave or on the hob in a saucepan so that it is above room temperature. Slowly add the lukewarm milk to the flour and butter mixture, mixing to form a soft, sticky dough. Don't overwork the mixture or the scones will lose their lightness.

Use the ice-cream scoop to portion out your rock cake scones on the prepared baking sheets, leaving a 5-cm/2-inch gap either side for expansion. Each one should be about the size of a small clementine. Brush the top of each rock cake scone with the beaten egg and then sprinkle with the soft dark brown sugar.

Bake in the preheated oven for 20 minutes until lightly golden brown on the top.

Serve these warm with homemade jam and clotted cream and everyone will love you!

gluten-free bakewell traybake

This easy traybake is our version of the classic British bakewell tart, but without the need to make pastry and a frangipane filling. You can easily use the basic gluten-free sponge recipe here to make any flavour of traybake you fancy – we suggest you swap the cherries and almonds for our Candied Chilli Pineapple (see page 37) for a tropical twist.

DIFFICULTY	MAKES 9	PREP TIME 25 MINUTES	BAKE TIME 40–50 MINUTES

250 g/2¼ sticks unsalted butter, softened

250 g/1¼ cups caster/granulated sugar

5 eggs

1 teaspoon vanilla bean paste

1 teaspoon almond extract

65 g/½ cup gluten-free plain/all-purpose flour

190 g/scant 2 cups ground almonds

½ teaspoon baking powder

½ teaspoon xanthan gum

200 g/7 oz. pitted fresh cherries, halved

100 g/1¼ cups flaked/slivered almonds

23-cm/9-inch square cake pan or a 25-cm/10-inch round cake pan, base-lined with greaseproof baking parchment

Preheat the oven to 190°C/fan 170°C (375°F) Gas 5.

Put the butter and sugar in a mixing bowl. Beat together at a medium speed with a hand-held electric whisk (or use a stand mixer with the paddle attachment) until pale and fluffy.

Add the eggs, vanilla bean paste and almond extract and mix until combined. Don't worry if the mixture looks like it is curdling at this point, it will come together.

Add the gluten-free flour, ground almonds, baking powder and xanthan gum. Beat it all together just until well combined.

Scoop all the mixture into the prepared square or round cake pan of your choice and spread level with a spatula. Dot the sponge mixture with the cherry halves and sprinkle over the flaked/slivered almonds.

Bake in the preheated oven for 40–50 minutes until golden brown on top and a skewer inserted into the middle comes out clean.

Leave to cool in the pan, then cut into nine squares or portions. This is gorgeous served slightly warm with vanilla ice cream for dessert or served cold for afternoon tea.

butterscotch biskies

What could be better than this version of our signature bake in chocolate and butterscotch? The light, buttery caramel combined with chocolate is a luscious flavour combination that everyone will want to try.

DIFFICULTY   **MAKES 12–15**   **PREP TIME 2½ HOURS +**   **BAKE TIME 10–15 MINUTES**
CHILL TIME

CHOCOLATE BISKIE DOUGH

85 g/3 oz. Chocolate Crumb
   (see page 13)
125 g/1⅛ sticks unsalted butter,
   softened
70 g/⅓ cup plus 1 teaspoon caster/
   granulated sugar
70 g/⅓ cup soft light brown sugar
1 teaspoon baking powder
1 teaspoon fine salt
2 eggs, at room temperature
50 g/2½ tablespoons golden/
   light corn syrup
60 g/2¼ oz. milk chocolate,
   melted and cooled
140 g/1 cup plus 1 tablespoon
   plain/all-purpose flour
10 g/1¼ tablespoons cocoa powder

TO ASSEMBLE

1 x batch Butterscotch Sauce
   (see page 22)
1 x batch Biskie Buttercream
   (see page 16)
demerara/turbinado sugar,
   for sprinkling

*piping/pastry bag with a plain nozzle/
tip and a small 10-point star-
shaped nozzle/tip (2-cm/¾-inch)*

Prepare the chocolate crumb and set aside to cool.

Put the softened butter, both sugars, baking powder and salt in a mixing bowl. Beat together at a high speed using a hand-held electric whisk (or the paddle attachment in a stand mixer) until light and fluffy. Scrape down the sides of the bowl and add the eggs and golden/light corn syrup. Beat for 10 minutes at a medium speed until it resembles thick yogurt.

Add the cooled melted chocolate and chocolate crumb and sift in the flour and cocoa. Beat in slowly at first, then at a medium speed for 1-2 minutes until combined. Pop the mixture into a container, cover and refrigerate for 1 hour.

Preheat the oven to 180°C/fan 160°C (350°F) Gas 4.

Scoop out 20 g/¾ oz. portions of the mix. Roll into balls and space out over two non-stick baking sheets with 4-cm/1½-inch gaps each side. Bake in the preheated oven for 10–15 minutes until slightly darker. Transfer to a cooling rack to cool.

Make a batch of butterscotch sauce and leave to cool. Prepare a batch of biskie buttercream. Mix 200 g/7 oz. of the cooled butterscotch into the buttercream until well combined, reserving the rest of the butterscotch. Transfer three quarters of the buttercream to the piping/pastry bag with the plain nozzle/tip. Pipe a spiral of buttercream onto half the biskies and then drizzle over a teaspoon of the reserved butterscotch. These will be the bases. Refrigerate for 20 minutes to set.

Meanwhile, place the remaining buttercream in the piping/pastry bag with the star nozzle/tip and pipe a small star onto each of the remaining biskies (the tops). Sprinkle with demerara/turbinado sugar and finish with a drizzle of butterscotch. Place the tops on the bottoms and serve.

raspberry ripple layer cake

This crowd-pleasing cake pays homage to the classic Victoria sponge. Our vanilla bean buttercream and the tart raspberry jam give it extra va-va-voom.

DIFFICULTY 🥄🥄🥄🥄🥄 **SERVES 12–14** | **PREP TIME 2½ HOURS +** **CHILL TIME** | **BAKE TIME 25–30 MINUTES**

1 x batch 20-cm/8-inch Vanilla Cake Batter (see page 11)

1 x batch Raspberry Jam (see page 21)

1½ x batches Light as a Feather Buttercream (see page 16)

30 g/4 teaspoons vanilla bean paste

1 x batch Vanilla Syrup (see page 19)

TO DECORATE

20 g/¾ oz. freeze-dried raspberry powder, sifted if there are seeds and mixed to a paste with 2 teaspoons cold water

150 g/5½ oz. fresh raspberries

3 x 20-cm/8-inch cake pans, base-lined with greaseproof baking parchment

piping/pastry bag with a large plain 2.5-cm/1-inch nozzle/tip and a small 5-point star-shaped nozzle/tip

cake board or cake stand

cake scraper

offset spatula

Preheat the oven to 180°C/fan 160°C (350°F) Gas 4.

Prepare a batch of the 20-cm/8-inch vanilla cake batter and divide between the three cake pans. Bake in the preheated oven following the instructions on page 11.

When cool, trim the sponges to flat, even layers. Cut each sponge in half horizontally so that you have six thin layers.

Prepare the raspberry jam and let cool. Prepare the light as a feather buttercream and mix in the vanilla paste. Transfer half of the buttercream to the piping/pastry bag with the large plain nozzle/tip, reserving the rest. Prepare the vanilla syrup.

Line the sides of one of the pans that you baked the sponges in with a double layer of greaseproof baking parchment, about 15 cm/6 inches high. Put the first sponge in and drizzle over 65 ml/generous ¼ cup of the warm vanilla syrup. Pipe on 100 g/3½ oz. buttercream and smooth out evenly. Spoon on a fifth of the raspberry jam and spread evenly. Add the next sponge and repeat the process with the syrup, buttercream and jam. Drizzle the top layer with syrup, then smooth over 2 tablespoons of buttercream. Freeze the cake for 20 minutes or refrigerate for 40 minutes to set.

Remove the pan and paper and transfer the cake to a board or cake stand with a blob of buttercream underneath. Swirl the raspberry paste very lightly into the reserved buttercream. Transfer to the piping/pastry bag and pipe rings of buttercream around the cake from the bottom up to cover. Smooth the buttercream around the sides of the cake using the cake scraper, cleaning it as you go. Use an offset spatula to scrape any overspill onto the top of the cake and smooth over to cover the top. Switch to the star-shaped nozzle/tip and pipe 12 buttercream peaks on top. Decorate with fresh raspberries.

vegan toffee apple cupcakes

We make little loaf cake versions of these cupcakes for our customers and they go down a storm. Just like our Vegan Cauldron Cupcakes (see page 69), there is no giveaway that these are vegan. The tartness of the fresh apple jam centre balances out the toffee-smothered moist sponge.

| DIFFICULTY | MAKES 12 | PREP TIME 50 MINUTES | BAKE TIME 25 MINUTES |

VEGAN VANILLA SPONGE
490 g/3⅔ cups plain/
   all-purpose flour
2 teaspoons baking powder
2 teaspoons bicarbonate of soda/
   baking soda
1 teaspoon fine salt
450 g/2¼ cups caster/
   granulated sugar
160 ml/generous ⅔ cup
   vegetable oil
35 ml/2¼ tablespoons apple
   cider vinegar
2 teaspoons vanilla bean paste

VEGAN CARAMEL
300 g/1½ cups soft light brown
   sugar
300 ml/1¼ cups coconut milk

TO DECORATE
1 x batch Apple Jam (see page 21)
1 tart green eating apple, such as
   Granny Smith
freshly squeezed juice of 1 lemon

12 large cupcake cases
12-hole cupcake pan

Preheat the oven to 190°C/fan 170°C (375°F) Gas 5.

For the vegan sponge, sift all the dry ingredients into a mixing bowl and stir together. Mix all the wet ingredients together with 300 ml/1¼ cups water and slowly add to the dry ingredients, mixing in until combined.

Divide the mixture between the 12 cupcake cases in the cupcake pan. Bake in the preheated oven for 25 minutes until the sponges are risen and set. Leave to cool.

For the vegan caramel, put the soft light brown sugar into a saucepan over a low-medium heat. Heat for a few minutes, stirring, until half melted. Add the coconut milk and boil for 10 minutes until slightly thickened. Leave to cool.

Meanwhile, prepare the apple jam and leave to cool.

Halve and core the apple for the decoration and slice it as thinly as possible into half-moon shapes, then slice again into small triangles. Toss in the lemon juice to stop any browning and set aside.

To assemble, use a small, sharp knife to cut small circular holes out of the middle of the cupcakes, keeping the little circles of sponge that you cut out. Fill the holes in the cupcakes with a spoonful of the apple jam, followed by a generous spoonful of the vegan caramel; it's fine if it spills out of the tops.

Place the cut-out cake pieces back on top of the cakes and stick an apple slice into the caramel to decorate.

strawberry cake truffles

These cake truffles are a great way to use up any scraps of cake sponge
you have leftover. It is amazing how much flavour is packed into them.

DIFFICULTY 🥄   MAKES 10–12   PREP TIME 45 MINUTES + CHILL TIME   BAKE TIME N/A

200 g/7 oz. leftover vanilla cake
sponge (or ½ batch 15-cm/
6-inch Vanilla Cake Batter,
(see page 11)
200 g/7 oz. Vanilla Crumb
(see page 13)
85 g/3 oz. Strawberry Jam
(see page 21)
10 g/¼ oz. freeze-dried strawberry
powder
100 g/3½ oz. white chocolate,
melted

*large tray or plate lined with
greaseproof baking parchment*

Prepare the vanilla cake batter (if needed) and bake in one
pan for 20–25 minutes. Prepare the vanilla crumb and then
the strawberry jam, following the instructions in the basic
recipes. Set all aside to cool.

Using your hands, finely crumble the cake sponge
into a mixing bowl. Mix in the jam with a wooden spoon to
form a dough-like mixture. Roll the mixture into 10–12 balls
(the size of ping pong balls), then place on the prepared tray
or plate and refrigerate for 30 minutes until firm.

In a food processor, blitz the vanilla crumb with the
strawberry powder. Dip each cake truffle into the melted
white chocolate and turn to cover them completely, then roll
in the strawberry crumb to coat. Refrigerate for 10 minutes
until set. These will last for a good week stored in an airtight
container in the fridge.

vegan aquafaba pavlovas

These mini vegan meringues are kitchen magic at its finest! The cooking liquid from chickpeas, known as 'aquafaba', is used instead of egg whites. We have found that organic jarred chickpeas work best, but you can use canned. Add coconut cream and berries and you'll be in pavlova heaven!

DIFFICULTY 🥄🥄🥄   **MAKES 12**   **PREP TIME 40 MINUTES +** **BAKE TIME 50 MINUTES**
CHILL TIME

150 ml/⅔ cup chickpea liquid (aquafaba) ideally from a jar (or can) organic cooked chickpeas
150 g/¾ cup caster/superfine sugar
¼ teaspoon beetroot/beet powder, plus a little extra, to decorate

TO SERVE
2 x 400 g/14 oz. cans coconut milk, with at least 75% coconut cream
500 g/1 lb. 2 oz. fresh mixed berries, such as raspberries, blackberries and blueberries

2 baking sheets, lined with greaseproof baking parchment

Preheat the oven to 140°C/fan 120°C (275°F) Gas 1.

Place the cans of coconut milk in the fridge to chill for at least 1 hour before using later.

Place the chickpea liquid into a saucepan and bring to the boil. Turn off the heat and leave to cool completely. (Boiling aquafaba before use makes for a more stable meringue.)

Place the chickpea liquid into a mixing bowl. Whisk with a hand-held electric whisk (or use a stand mixer with the whisk attachment) at a high speed for about 5–10 minutes until it turns white and has soft peaks. Slowly add the sugar while whisking, a tablespoon at a time, until the meringue is glossy and a bit stiffer; it won't whip to stiff peaks like egg whites do.

Sprinkle in the beetroot/beet powder and fold in lightly to make pink streaks. Spoon 6 heaps of meringue on each prepared baking sheet. Use the back of the spoon to make an indent for the cream and fruit to nestle in on each one.

Bake in the preheated oven for 50 minutes until crisp and dry. Leave to cool completely in the oven with the door ajar.

When you are ready to serve, drain and discard the water from the chilled cans of coconut milk. Scoop the cream out, place into a bowl and mix until smooth. Spoon a tablespoon of coconut cream onto each meringue and top with fresh fruit; we have chosen raspberries, blackberries and blueberries. Sprinkle with a little extra beetroot/beet powder to decorate.

TIP These pavlovas can be assembled about 10 minutes ahead of time, but as they are fragile, you can't leave them too long or the moisture from the cream will melt them!

pink lemonade

Straight out of our Hello Kitty's Secret Garden Afternoon Tea, everyone loved the cute but natural light pink colour of this lemonade. It's not too sweet, and its freshness makes this drink the perfect summer cooler. Don't worry, you won't taste the beetroot/beet!

200 g/1 cup caster/granulated sugar
200 ml/generous ¾ cup freshly squeezed
　lemon juice
1 teaspoon beetroot/beet powder
ice
1 litre/quart chilled soda water

TO GARNISH
lemon slices
4 fresh mint sprigs

4 highball or tall glasses
4 straws

SERVES 4

Put the caster/granulated sugar, lemon juice and beetroot/beet powder in a jug/pitcher and mix well to dissolve the sugar and powder.

Divide the mixture between your four serving glasses, add ice and top up with soda water (the ratio should be about 2 parts soda water to 1 part lemon mixture). Stir each glass.

Serve each with lemon slices, a sprig of fresh mint and a straw.

london fog tea latte

This drink is a best seller in our stores. 'London' is a reference to the Earl Grey tea blend and 'fog' refers to the cloudy finish from the frothed milk. Tea lattes are impressive, but so easy to make! You don't need a milk frother, a whisk and saucepan will do the trick, but if you do have one, then you can use that instead and give your arm a rest.

1 teabag or teaspoon Earl Grey loose leaf tea
500 ml/2 cups plus 2 tablespoons boiling water
1 teaspoon Vanilla Syrup (see page 19)
250 ml/1 cup plus 1 tablespoon milk of your
　choice
edible flowers or finely grated lemon zest,
　to garnish (optional)

SERVES 2

Brew the Earl Grey in the boiling water for 3–4 minutes. Remove the teabag (if needed) or strain and mix in the vanilla syrup.

Pour into two large, heatproof serving glasses or mugs.

Heat the milk in a saucepan until steaming and whisk vigorously to make it foamy. Top each Earl Grey tea with the hot milk and foam. Decorate with edible flowers or grated lemon zest.

THE ORIENT
afternoon tea

Our oriental roots really come through in this
chapter. Many of these recipes are new inventions
and we can't wait for you to try them out!

vegan curry puffs

Even if you are not vegan, these are a MUST try! The divinely crisp vegan pastry provides the perfect vessel for the punchy potato and spinach curry filling. You can make any shape you like, but the triangle shape is our homage to Chinese puff pastries usually served in dim sum.

DIFFICULTY 🥄🥄🥄 | **MAKES 8** | **PREP TIME 40 MINUTES +** **CHILL TIME** | **BAKE TIME 25 MINUTES**

1 x batch Vegan Rough Puff Pastry (see page 15)

1 tablespoon vegetable oil

1 medium potato (a fluffy variety like Maris Piper or baking potato), peeled and cut into small cubes

1 shallot or ½ medium onion, roughly chopped

½ tomato, roughly chopped

1 handful fresh spinach leaves

1½ teaspoons medium curry powder

pinch of ground cinnamon

1 garlic clove, peeled and finely chopped

½ teaspoon freshly ground black pepper

1 teaspoon fine salt

1 tablespoon coconut cream block, roughly chopped (optional)

plain/all-purpose flour, for dusting the work surface

a little vegan milk of your choice, for glazing

Prepare the vegan rough puff pastry and chill in the fridge.

Put the oil, potato, shallot or onion, tomato, spinach, curry powder, cinnamon, garlic, black pepper and salt into a saucepan and cook over a medium heat for about 20 minutes, stirring occasionally, until the potato is nearly fully cooked.

Meanwhile, remove the pastry from the fridge and let it warm up for 10 minutes until soft enough to roll out.

Add the coconut cream pieces (if using) to the potato mixture, let them melt and then mix in until fully combined. Set the mixture aside to cool.

Cut the pastry roughly in half. Roll out one half on a lightly floured work surface to a rectangle about 40 x 10-cm/16 x 4-inches; with a thickness of about 0.5-cm/¼-inch. Cut the pastry into four 10 x 10-cm/4 x 4-inch squares.

Divide the cooled potato filling into eight portions and shape into balls. Place a ball of filling into the middle of a pastry square. Wet two edges of the pastry (to help it stick) and fold one corner over the mixture to meet the opposite corner and make a triangle. Carefully pinch along the join to ensure the mixture does not leak out. Trim any excess pastry away to make neat edges. Repeat with the remaining pastry squares, then the other pastry half and filling to make eight.

Space the curry puffs out over two non-stick baking sheets and brush the tops with vegan milk of your choice for a shiny brown finish. Pop into the fridge to chill for 10 minutes.

Preheat the oven to 200°C/fan 180°C (400°F) Gas 6.

Bake the puffs in the preheated oven for 25 minutes until lightly golden brown. These are delicious served warm or cold.

mini vegetable spring rolls

Spring rolls are the classic oriental appetizer! You won't find a filo/phyllo pastry recipe in this book because, frankly, life is too short! What makes these little spring rolls so great is that you don't need a deep-fat fryer, but you still get that satisfying crispy flaky shell.

DIFFICULTY ✎ | **MAKES 12** | **PREP TIME 20 MINUTES** | **BAKE TIME 12 MINUTES**

---

200 g/7 oz. mixed stir-fry
  vegetables of your choice
  (ideally including bamboo
  shoots and water chestnuts)
1 tablespoon vegetable oil,
  plus extra for brushing
1 garlic clove, peeled and crushed
2 tablespoons hoisin sauce
2 pinches fine salt
2 pinches freshly ground black
  pepper
1 pack (270 g/9½ oz.) filo/
  phyllo pastry
1 tablespoon black sesame seeds

TO SERVE
sliced spring onions/scallions
mayonnaise mixed with Sriracha
  hot sauce to taste

Preheat the oven to 220°C/fan 200°C (425°F) Gas 7.

Use a sharp knife to finely shred the mixed stir-fry vegetables, making sure that no piece is longer than 5-cm/2-inches in length as these spring rolls are small.

Put a frying pan/skillet over a high heat and add the vegetable oil. When the oil is hot, add the shredded vegetables and garlic and stir-fry for 2 minutes. Add the hoisin sauce, salt and pepper and stir-fry for 1 minute more. Transfer to a bowl and leave to cool.

Cut the filo/phyllo pastry into twenty-four 15 x 10-cm/6 x 4-inch small rectangular sheets. Dampen a clean kitchen cloth or kitchen paper and cover the pastry sheets to stop them drying out. Position one sheet in front of you with the long side nearest you. Brush both sides of the pastry liberally with vegetable oil, stack another sheet on top facing the same way and brush with oil again. Place about a tablespoonful of the filling neatly down the centre of the sheet horizontally, leaving a gap of about 1 cm/½-inch at each end. Take the long edge of pastry nearest you and roll it halfway over the filling, pausing to quickly fold in both short ends, then roll all the way up. Place the roll on a baking sheet with the seam at the bottom. Repeat with the remaining pastry sheets and filling until all the spring rolls are made, then sprinkle with the sesame seeds.

Bake in the preheated oven for 12 minutes until golden brown. Serve the spring rolls hot, garnished with the sliced spring onions/scallions and with Sriracha mayonnaise on the side for dipping.

spring onion & sesame pancakes

Our grandmother made these for us when we were little. She used to tell us that patience was the secret: the hot water dough will change from a sticky mess to soft and elastic in about the same time as it takes to cool. The dough itself is quite plain so be generous with the seasonings.

DIFFICULTY 🥄🥄🥄 | **MAKES 6–7** | **PREP TIME 30 MINUTES** | **COOK TIME 4–6 MINUTES**

200 g/1½ cups plain/
   all-purpose flour
2 tablespoons vegetable oil,
   plus extra for oiling the work
   surface and frying
100 ml/⅓ cup plus 1 tablespoon
   hot (not boiling) water (about
   60°C/140°F)
6–7 teaspoons sesame oil
6 spring onions/scallions,
   finely chopped
1 tablespoon rock salt
   (ideally Maldon)
1 tablespoon freshly ground
   black pepper
6–7 teaspoons toasted sesame
   seeds
your favourite sweet chilli/chili
   sauce, for dipping
handful of fresh coriander/
   cilantro, to garnish (optional)

Put the flour, vegetable oil and hot water into a bowl and mix until it forms a ball. Knead the dough either in the bowl or on a lightly oiled surface for about 5 minutes until it is cold; it will be soft and elastic.

Form the dough into a long sausage approx. 5 cm/2 inches in diameter. Slice into 6–7 pieces and roughly shape into balls.

Heavily oil (don't flour) the work surface and roll one dough ball out into a thin pancake, with a thickness similar to a crêpe. You should just be able to see through it, but don't go any thinner than this. Spread 1 teaspoon of sesame oil onto the pancake to cover. Evenly sprinkle with 1 tablespoon finely chopped spring onions/scallions followed by a very generous pinch each of salt and pepper. Finally, sprinkle with 1 teaspoon of toasted sesame seeds. Roll the pancake up like a Swiss roll/jelly roll, then curl the roll into a spiral – this is how the flaky layers are made. Flatten the spiral a little with your hand, then lightly roll it out again into a thick pancake; don't worry if it splits a little. Repeat the same steps for the remaining dough balls and filling to make 6–7 thick pancakes.

Rub a large, cold frying pan/skillet with some oil so it is lightly coated, then set over a medium heat. Cook each pancake for 2–3 minutes on each side until lightly golden brown. Press down on the edges with a spatula as they are frying to help them cook.

Serve these pancakes hot, cut into quarters with sweet chilli/chili sauce for dipping. Garnish with fresh coriander/cilantro, if you like. They can be reheated in a frying pan/skillet over a medium heat for 1 minute if needed.

savoury spiced biscuits

These are the most ridiculously moreish bites. They melt in the mouth and the spices give them a gentle savoury flavour, which makes it impossible to stop at one! You can buy decorative stamps, like the one we've used here, to adorn your biscuits, or just leave them plain and enjoy.

DIFFICULTY	MAKES ABOUT 20	PREP TIME 15 MINUTES + CHILL TIME	BAKE TIME 12 MINUTES

110 g/1 stick unsalted butter,
   at room temperature, cubed
50 g/¼ cup caster/granulated
   sugar
150 g/1 cup plus 2 tablespoons
   plain/all-purpose flour
½ teaspoon medium curry powder
½ teaspoon paprika
½ teaspoon ground turmeric
¼ teaspoon cayenne pepper
   or chilli/chili powder
¼ teaspoon fine salt
¼ teaspoon freshly ground
   black pepper

*2 baking sheets, lined with
   greaseproof baking parchment*
decorative cookie stamp (optional)

Put the butter and sugar in a mixing bowl or the bowl of a stand mixer and cream together using a hand-held electric whisk or the paddle attachment until pale and fluffy.

Sift the flour, curry powder, all the other spices and salt and pepper into a separate bowl and mix together. Add to the butter and sugar mixture and mix in until well blended and the mixture comes together into a dough.

Divide the dough in half and roll each piece into a long neat sausage about 3 cm/1¼ inches in diameter – you can do this in clingfilm/plastic wrap, which makes it easier. Wrap each one in clingfilm/plastic wrap if you haven't already and chill in the fridge for at least 30 minutes until firm.

Preheat the oven to 180°C/fan 160°C (350°F) Gas 4.

When the dough is cold and firm, unwrap and cut 5-mm/¼-inch slices off each sausage and space them out on the prepared baking sheets. If desired, allow the dough to warm up slightly until soft to the touch and stamp with a decorative cookie stamp to leave a pretty pattern. If the dough sticks to the stamp, very gently prise it off so as not to tear the dough.

Bake in the preheated oven for 12 minutes until lightly golden. Transfer to a cooling rack to cool before serving.

TIP If you want to make the dough ahead, it will last for up to 3 days in the fridge wrapped in clingfilm/plastic wrap. You can also freeze it and keep for up to 1 month (defrost to fridge temperature to use).

miso caramel madeleines

Our recipe gives classic French madeleines an oriental twist! While miso is mostly associated with soup and black cod, combined with soft brown sugar, butter and vanilla, it transforms into a 'can't quite work out what that delicious flavour is' cake bite. These are great warm out of the oven, or box them up and give them as a gift on the same day as baking. The recipe is so easy you will want to keep making them over and over.

DIFFICULTY 🥄	MAKES 12	PREP TIME 10 MINUTES + REST TIME	BAKE TIME 15 MINUTES

100 g/1 stick minus 1 tablespoon
   unsalted butter
2 UK large/US extra-large eggs
100 g/½ cup soft light brown
   sugar
30 g/2½ tablespoons caster/
   granulated sugar
80 g/⅔ cup minus 1 tablespoon
   plain/all-purpose flour
30 g/⅓ cup ground almonds
½ teaspoon baking powder
30 g/1 oz. white miso paste
1 teaspoon vanilla bean paste
20 g/1 tablespoon plus
   2 teaspoons demerara/
   turbinado sugar, to coat

*12-hole madeleine pan or silicone
   mould, greased with butter*

Put the butter into a small saucepan and melt, then remove from the heat and leave to cool.

Combine the eggs, soft light brown sugar, caster/granulated sugar, flour, ground almonds, baking powder, white miso paste and vanilla bean paste together in a large bowl and mix together with a spatula until well combined.

Add the cooled melted butter and mix well. Leave the mixture to rest for 20 minutes at room temperature.

Preheat the oven to 180°C/fan 160°C (350°F) Gas 4. Fill each hole in the greased pan or mould to the top with the mixture and bake in the preheated oven for 15 minutes until risen and golden.

Leave to cool a little, then pop the madeleines out of their moulds and dip in the demerara/turbinado sugar to coat while they are still warm. These are best eaten when freshly made.

black sesame sandwich cookies

These are a revelation! Black sesame is a common flavouring in the Far East in hot and cold desserts, and we use it in many of our bakes. The toasted black sesame gives these cookies a light nutty flavour without adding any heaviness. You can serve these without the chocolate filling if you are short on time – but it does make them even more delicious!

DIFFICULTY ◗◗◗   **MAKES 12**   **PREP TIME 35 MINUTES + CHILL TIME**   **BAKE TIME 12 MINUTES**

85 g/3 oz. black sesame seeds
250 g/2¼ sticks unsalted butter, softened
175 g/¾ cup plus 2 tablespoons caster/granulated sugar
175 g/¾ cup plus 2 tablespoons soft light brown sugar
2 eggs
2 teaspoons vanilla bean paste
285 g/2 cups plus 2 tablespoons plain/all-purpose flour
1 teaspoon fine salt
1½ teaspoons baking powder

CHOCOLATE GANACHE FILLING
140 ml/scant ⅔ cup double/ heavy cream
200 g/7 oz. milk chocolate, broken into pieces

2 baking sheets, lined with greaseproof baking parchment
piping/pastry bag with a 2-cm/ ¾-inch star-shaped nozzle/tip

Put the black sesame seeds in a small, dry frying pan/skillet over a medium heat and toast, shaking the pan occasionally, for about 10 minutes until you hear them pop. Tip the seeds into a food processor and blitz to a fine paste. Set aside.

Preheat the oven to 200°C/fan 180°C (400°F) Gas 6.

Put the butter and both sugars in a mixing bowl and cream together at a medium speed using a hand-held electric whisk (or the paddle attachment in a stand mixer). When creamed, whisk in the eggs, one by one, followed by the vanilla. Sift in the flour, salt and baking powder, then add the sesame paste. Mix until a dough forms.

Divide the dough into twenty-four 20 g/¾ oz. portions and roll into balls. Space the balls out on the prepared baking sheets and bake in the preheated oven for 12 minutes until they are slightly brown at the edges. Cool the cookies on a cooling rack ready for sandwiching!

Meanwhile, for the ganache filling, put the double/heavy cream into a saucepan and heat over a medium heat until steaming. Place the broken milk chocolate in a heatproof bowl and quickly pour over the hot cream. Stir into a smooth ganache. Leave to set for about 30 minutes at room temperature until thick and pipeable.

Pop into the piping/pastry bag with the star-shaped nozzle/ tip and pipe a star on top of 12 of the cookies. Place the other cookies on top and serve.

yuzu & lemon egg custard tart

Yuzu is one of our favourite fruits; if you haven't tried it before it's like
a sweeter, more fragrant lemon. Like any egg tart, this recipe takes a little
concentration and bravery, but it is completely worth the result!

DIFFICULTY ✎✎✎✎ | **SERVES 14** | **PREP TIME 1 HOUR +** CHILL TIME | **BAKE TIME 1 HOUR** 20–30 MINUTES

1 x batch Sweet Shortcrust Pastry
   (see page 14)
plain/all-purpose flour,
   for dusting the work surface
1 egg, beaten
icing/confectioners' sugar and
   softly whipped cream (optional),
   to serve

YUZU & LEMON CUSTARD
1 egg
9 egg yolks
130 g/⅔ cup caster/
   granulated sugar
50 ml/3½ tablespoons freshly
   squeezed lemon juice
50 ml/3½ tablespoons yuzu juice
400 ml/scant 1¾ cups double/
   heavy cream

*25-cm/10-inch non-stick tart pan
   with fluted edges
baking beans or dry raw rice*

Prepare the sweet shortcrust pastry and chill in the fridge.
Remove from the fridge 10 minutes before using so that it
is soft enough to work with. Roll the pastry out on a lightly
floured surface to 2-mm/1/16-inch thick, then lay it over the
tart pan; if it breaks a bit, just press it together again. Press
the pastry into the pan and leave it hanging slightly over the
edges. Prick all over the base, then refrigerate for 30 minutes.

Preheat the oven to 200°C/fan 180°C (400°F) Gas 6.

Cover the pastry with greaseproof baking parchment
and fill right to the edges with baking beans or dry raw rice.
Blind-bake in the preheated oven for 25 minutes.

Once baked, remove the paper and beans/rice. Brush the
pastry with the beaten egg and bake again for 15 minutes; this
will ensure no soggy bottom. Once baked, use a serrated knife
to trim off the excess pastry while still in the pan. Set aside.
Reduce the oven heat to 150°C/fan 130°C (300°F) Gas 2.

In a separate bowl, combine the 1 whole egg and 9 egg
yolks with the sugar and whisk together well. Add the lemon
and yuzu juices and stir in. Heat the cream in a saucepan until
steaming, then slowly pour into the egg mixture, whisking
quickly and constantly to combine until smooth.

Place the pastry case, still in the pan, in the oven on a
baking sheet and pour in the egg custard mixture all the way
to the top. Bake in the preheated oven for 40–50 minutes
until set but with a slight wobble in the centre.

Leave to cool completely in the pan before removing.
Dust with icing/confectioners' sugar and serve with some
softly whipped cream.

mango & passion fruit biskies

In these popular biskies, our special light buttercream is spiked with passion fruit syrup and combined with mango compote for a uniquely delicious treat.

DIFFICULTY 🥄🥄🥄🥄 **MAKES 12–15** | **PREP TIME 2½ HOURS + CHILL TIME** | **BAKE TIME 10–15 MINUTES**

VANILLA BISKIE DOUGH
85 g/¾ cup Vanilla Crumb
  (see page 13)
125 g/1⅛ sticks unsalted butter,
  softened
70 g/⅓ cup plus 1 teaspoon caster/
  granulated sugar
70 g/⅓ cup plus 1 teaspoon soft
  light brown sugar
1 teaspoon baking powder
1 teaspoon fine salt
2 eggs, at room temperature
50 g/¼ cup golden/corn syrup
1 teaspoon vanilla bean paste
170 g/1¼ cups plain/all-purpose
  flour

MANGO COMPOTE
200 g/7 oz. chopped fresh mango
1 teaspoon fresh lemon juice
50 g/¼ cup caster/granulated
  sugar

TO ASSEMBLE
1 x batch Biskie Buttercream
  (see page 16)
1 x batch Passion Fruit Syrup
  (see page 19)
100 g/3½ oz. melted white
  chocolate
dried mango slices and edible
  flowers, to decorate

*piping/pastry bag with a round
  plain 2-cm/¾-inch nozzle/tip*

Prepare the vanilla crumb and set aside to cool.

Put the softened butter, both sugars, baking powder and salt in a mixing bowl. Beat together at a medium speed with a hand-held electric whisk (or use a stand mixer with the paddle attachment) until light and fluffy.

Scrape down the sides of the bowl and add the eggs and golden/corn syrup. Beat for 10 minutes at a medium speed until well combined – it should resemble thick yogurt.

Add the vanilla paste and vanilla crumb and sift in the flour. Beat in slowly at first, then at a medium speed for 1–2 minutes until well combined. Pop the mixture into a container, cover and refrigerate for about 1 hour until firm.

Preheat the oven to 180°C/fan 160°C (350°F) Gas 4. Scoop out 20 g/¾ oz. portions of the mixture and roll into balls. Space the balls out on two non-stick baking sheets, leaving a 4-cm/1½-inch gap either side as they will spread. Bake in the preheated oven for 10–15 minutes until golden at the edges. Transfer to a cooling rack to cool.

Meanwhile, prepare the biskie buttercream, then add the cooled passion fruit syrup and beat together.

For the compote, mix the chopped mango, lemon juice and sugar together and set aside.

Transfer the buttercream to the piping/pastry bag with the 2-cm/¾-inch nozzle/tip and pipe two rings of buttercream, one on top of the other, on the flat side of each biskie. Fill the centres of half the biskies with the mango compote and sandwich the tops gently onto the bottoms. Drizzle the melted white chocolate over the tops of the biskies, and decorate each one with a dried mango slice and edible flowers.

matcha & strawberry melting moments

All across the Far East you will find every kind of sweet treat flavoured
with matcha green tea. These delicious matcha green tea cookies are
sandwiched together with a fresh strawberry and white chocolate
ganache filling; the sweetness complements the matcha beautifully.

DIFFICULTY 🥄🥄🥄　　　MAKES 20　　　PREP TIME 40 MINUTES +　BAKE TIME 10 MINUTES
　　　　　　　　　　　　　　　　　　　　　　　　　CHILL TIME

MATCHA COOKIES
250 g/2¼ sticks unsalted
　butter, softened
50 g/¼ cup caster/
　granulated sugar
50 g/generous ⅓ cup icing/
　confectioners' sugar
1 teaspoon vanilla bean paste
230 g/1¾ cups plain/
　all-purpose flour
25 g/¼ cup cornflour/cornstarch
20 g/¾ oz. matcha powder

STRAWBERRY GANACHE
100 g/3½ oz. fresh or frozen
　strawberries
2 teaspoons freshly squeezed
　lemon juice
¼ teaspoon beetroot/beet powder
200 g/7 oz. white chocolate,
　broken into pieces

*2 baking sheets, lined with
　greaseproof baking parchment
disposable piping/pastry bag*

Preheat the oven to 190°C/fan 170°C (375°F) Gas 5.

For the cookies, put the softened butter, caster/granulated
sugar and icing/confectioners' sugar in a mixing bowl. Cream
together at a medium-high speed with a hand-held electric
whisk (or use a stand mixer with the paddle attachment) until
light and fluffy.

Add the vanilla bean paste and mix in. Sift in the flour,
cornflour/cornstarch and 15 g/½ oz. of the matcha powder
(reserving the rest for decoration) and mix until combined
into a soft dough. Divide the dough into 40 balls and space
half out across the prepared baking sheets (you will need to
bake these in two batches of 20). Use a fork to flatten each
ball slightly on the baking sheet slightly, leaving an indentation
from the fork. Bake in the preheated oven for 10 minutes
until baked through and very light brown at the edges.
Transfer to a cooling rack and then bake the remaining
dough in the same way on the same baking sheets. Let cool.

To make the strawberry ganache filling, blitz the
strawberries to a smooth purée in a food processor, then add
the lemon juice and blitz again to combine. Put the strawberry
purée in a saucepan over a medium heat and heat until
steaming (but not boiling). Turn off the heat and mix in the
beetroot/beet powder. Add the white chocolate and stir until
smooth and combined. Leave to cool until pipeable.

Transfer the strawberry ganache to the piping/pastry bag
and cut a small hole in the end. Pipe ganache onto the flat side
of 20 of the cookies and sandwich together with the other
cookies. Dust with the remaining matcha powder to serve.

coconut dream cake

Our customers demand the return of this cake whenever we take it off the menu! The secret to the moist and light texture is the coconut soak.

DIFFICULTY 🥄🥄🥄🥄 **SERVES 12–15** | **PREP TIME 2½ HOURS + CHILL TIME** | **BAKE TIME 25–30 MINUTES**

1 x batch 20-cm/8-inch Vanilla Cake Batter (see page 11)
1½ x batches Light as a Feather Buttercream (see page 16)
210 g/7¼ oz. coconut cream block
1 x batch Coconut Ganache (see page 18)
1 x batch Coconut Soak (see page 19)
200 g/7 oz. dried coconut shavings/chips

3 x 20-cm/8-inch cake pans, greased and lined with greaseproof baking parchment
piping/pastry bag with a large plain 2.5-cm/1-inch nozzle/tip
cake stand or cake board
cake scraper
offset spatula

Preheat the oven to 180°C/fan 160°C (350°F) Gas 4.

Prepare the 20-cm/8-inch vanilla cake batter and divide between the three cake pans. Bake in the preheated oven following the instructions on page 11. Leave to cool in the pans for 5 minutes, then remove to a rack to cool completely.

When cool, trim the sponges to flat, even layers. Cut each sponge in half horizontally so that you have six thin layers.

Prepare 1½ batches of the light as a feather buttercream. Melt the coconut cream block in the microwave in 20-second bursts. Cool slightly and then mix into the buttercream slowly until well combined. Transfer to the piping/pastry bag with the 2.5-cm/1-inch nozzle/tip and set aside.

Prepare the coconut ganache and then the coconut soak. Line the sides of one of the pans that you baked the sponges in with a double layer of greaseproof baking parchment, about 15 cm/6 inches high. Put the first sponge in the pan and drizzle over 65 ml/generous ¼ cup of the warm coconut soak. Pipe about 100 g/3½ oz. buttercream on top smooth out into an even layer. Spread over a fifth of the ganache. Repeat the steps with the other sponges, coconut soak, buttercream and ganache until you get to the top layer. Drizzle coconut soak over and then smooth over 2 tablespoons of buttercream. Freeze the cake for 40 minutes or refrigerate for 1 hour.

Remove the pan and paper and transfer the cake to a board or cake stand with a blob of buttercream underneath. Pipe adjoining rings of buttercream around the sides of the cake to cover. Use the cake scraper to smooth around the sides of the cake, cleaning the scraper as you go. Use an offset spatula to scrape any overspill onto the top of the cake.

Finally, decorate the cake by pressing coconut shavings or chips all over the cake. It is now ready to serve!

raspberry & lychee no-bake cheesecake

Our father used to be famous for his no-bake lemon cheesecake and we
have happy childhood memories of helping him make the buttery, sugary
biscuit base – he used to give us a wine bottle to crush it all together!
Our own no-bake cheesecake, inspired by our Dad's, is great as it requires
NO baking and NO gelling agents and it looks and tastes stunning.

DIFFICULTY	SERVES 12–14	PREP TIME 30 MINUTES + CHILL TIME	BAKE TIME N/A

BASE
200 g/7 oz. digestive biscuits/
   graham crackers, crushed
175 g/1½ sticks unsalted butter,
   melted
50 g/¼ cup demerara/
   turbinado sugar

FILLING
400 g/14 oz. full-fat cream
   cheese
300 ml/1¼ cups double/heavy
   cream, whipped until stiff
100 g/¾ cup minus
   ½ tablespoon icing/
   confectioners' sugar
1 teaspoon rose water
200 g/7 oz. fresh raspberries
1 x 225 g/8 oz. can of lychees,
   well drained (or the same
   amount of peeled and pitted
   fresh lychees)
edible rose petals,
   to decorate

*20-cm/8-inch loose-bottomed cake
   pan, lined with clingfilm/plastic
   wrap (a spray of water inside the
   pan will help the plastic to stick)*

For the base, blitz the crushed biscuits/graham crackers
to fine crumbs in a food processor. Add the melted butter
and blitz again to combine. Transfer to a bowl and mix in the
demerara/turbinado sugar until well combined. Tip into the
bottom of the prepared cake pan, spread evenly and press
down firmly with your fingers until evenly compacted and
firm. Place in the fridge to harden for about 30 minutes.

Meanwhile, for the filling, put the cream cheese into a
clean bowl and mix just to loosen. Fold in the whipped cream,
icing/confectioners' sugar and rose water until well combined.
Finely chop 75 g/2⅔ oz. of the fresh raspberries, reserving the
rest and leaving them whole for the decoration. Reserve 6
lychees for decoration and finely chop the rest. Dry the
chopped lychees and chopped raspberries with some kitchen
paper to remove the excess juice and then mix lightly with the
cream mixture – do not overmix, you want a marbled effect.

Take the base from the fridge and spoon the cream cheese
mixture on top. Roughly smooth the surface with a spatula.
Freeze for 1–2 hours until firm but not frozen solid.

Remove the cheesecake from the pan and decorate by
placing the reserved whole lychees evenly around the top
edge, with whole raspberries and petals spaced in between.
Serve immediately.

matcha latte

The key to a silky smooth matcha latte is to really whisk the matcha and hot water together well. A special matcha whisk will do the job quickly, but a small normal whisk works too. Just like our other lattes, you can use a whisk and pan to froth your milk or a milk frother if you happen to have one.

300 ml/1¼ cups your favourite milk
1 teaspoon matcha powder, plus extra to serve
20 ml/1¼ tablespoons hot water

SERVES 1

Put your favourite milk into a saucepan and heat through until steaming. Whisk the hot milk vigorously until foamy. Set aside.

Place the matcha powder in a mug or latte glass, pour over the hot water and whisk together with a small whisk or a special matcha whisk (if you have one) into a smooth liquid.

Top up the mug or glass with the hot foamy milk. Dust with a little more matcha powder on top to garnish.

passion fruit, lychee & orange iced tea

This iced tea is known as our 'revive ice tea'; it takes three of our favourite fruits (oranges are lucky in the Chinese culture) and stirs them with a chilled fragrant jasmine green tea base to provide the perfect pick-me-up. This makes a nice mocktail, or you could even add a cheeky dash of vodka or lychee liqueur for a grown-up version.

2 jasmine green teabags
1 litre/quart hot water
ice
200 ml/generous ¾ cup Passion Fruit Syrup (see page 19)
1 x 225 g/8 oz. can lychees, drained
1 medium orange, cut into thin half slices

4 tall glass tumblers
straws

SERVES 4

Brew the jasmine green teabags in the hot water for 3–5 minutes. Remove the teabags, pour the tea into a large jug/pitcher and leave to cool.

When the tea is cool, add ice to each serving glass, followed by 3 tablespoons each of passion fruit syrup, two lychees and two slices of orange. Top up the glasses with the cold jasmine green tea. Add straws and serve.

AMERICANA
afternoon tea

Our American friends have introduced us to some incredible flavour combinations and bakes. We wanted to pay homage to our friends from across the pond with this collection of fun recipes.

bacon & sweetcorn muffins

Is there anything more American than a muffin? These are moist and crammed with delicious fried bacon and sweetcorn/corn, the spring onions (or scallions as Americans call them) add a lovely fresh bite. Oh, and did we mention there was bacon in these?! They are perfect for your afternoon tea, afternoon snack or even breakfast, why not?!

DIFFICULTY	MAKES 12	PREP TIME 10 MINUTES	BAKE TIME 12 MINUTES

½ teaspoon paprika
120 g/4¼ oz. cooked/fried smoked bacon lardons or chopped cooked streaky bacon (for a vegetarian substitution, use the same weight of mature/sharp Cheddar cheese or feta)
50 g/1¾ oz. drained canned sweetcorn/corn
50 g/1¾ oz. chopped spring onions/scallions
¼ teaspoon freshly ground black pepper
½ teaspoon fine salt
250 g/1¾ cups plus 2 tablespoons plain/all-purpose flour
1 tablespoon baking powder
250 ml/1 cup plus 1 tablespoon whole milk
50 g/3½ tablespoons unsalted butter, melted
1 UK large/US extra-large egg, beaten
cream cheese or salted butter, to serve (optional)

12-hole muffin pan, greased or lined with 12 muffin cases (optional)

Preheat the oven to 220°C/fan 200°C (425°F) Gas 7.

Stir together the paprika, cooked bacon (or cheese), sweetcorn/corn, spring onions/scallions, black pepper, salt, flour and baking powder in a large mixing bowl.

Add the milk, melted butter and egg and stir with a wooden spoon until well combined.

Divide the mixture equally between the 12-hole muffin pan (filling each hole about three quarters of the way up).

Bake in the preheated oven for 12 minutes until golden on the top.

If you aren't using cases, you may need to ease out the muffins with a palette knife, loosening around the edges.

These are best served warm and can be reheated in a hot oven for 5 minutes if needed.

Perfect served with some cream cheese or salted butter.

pizza pastry twists

We used to make these pizza pastry twists with our dad. The flavour combo is classic and kids will love them. If you are in a hurry, these would work well with pre-made puff pastry. The twists can be made into any size you like, just be generous with the tomato and fresh basil topping as it really gives an intense fresh pizza flavour.

DIFFICULTY	MAKES 10 LONG OR 20 SHORT TWISTS	PREP TIME 20 MINUTES + CHILL TIME	BAKE TIME 20 MINUTES

1 x batch Rough Puff Pastry (see page 15) or Vegan Rough Puff Pastry (see page 15)
8 tablespoons tomato purée/paste
2 teaspoons fine salt
1 teaspoon freshly ground black pepper
2 teaspoons dried oregano
4 garlic cloves, peeled and finely chopped or crushed
plain/all-purpose flour, for dusting the work surface
5–6 fresh basil sprigs, leaves removed and finely chopped
150 g/5½ oz. grated mature/sharp Cheddar cheese (or a vegan alternative)

Prepare the rough puff or vegan rough puff pastry and chill as instructed. Remove from the fridge 10 minutes before you want to use it so that it is soft enough to work with.

Put the tomato purée/paste, salt, pepper, oregano and garlic in a bowl and mix together.

Divide the pastry in half and roughly form one half into the shape of a rectangle. Roll out on a lightly floured surface to a large rectangle approx. 30 x 25 cm/12 x 10 inches.

Spread half the tomato mixture evenly all over the pastry right to the edges. Evenly sprinkle over half the chopped fresh basil, then half the grated cheese. Cut the pastry into five long equal strips lengthways or 10 short equal strips widthways.

Take both ends of one strip and twist together three times for a short twist or five times for a long twist; don't worry if some of the topping falls off. Repeat with the rest of the strips. Repeat the steps for the remaining pastry and topping.

Transfer all the twists to two non-stick baking sheets and sprinkle with any of the topping that has fallen off. Chill in the fridge for 10 minutes.

Preheat the oven to 200°C/fan 180°C (400°F) Gas 6.

Bake the twists the preheated oven for 20 minutes or until the cheese has browned and the pastry is lightly golden.

Leave to cool before serving.

vegan roasted sweet potato tarts

The fresh sprigs of rosemary and sliced chilli/chile nestled into the roasted sweet potatoes give these vegan tarts an impressive depth of flavour.

DIFFICULTY 🥄🥄🥄 | MAKES 4 | PREP TIME 50 MINUTES + CHILL TIME | BAKE TIME 20 MINUTES

1 x batch Vegan Rough Puff Pastry (see page 15)
150 g/5½ oz. (approx. 1–2 small) sweet potatoes, peeled and roughly chopped into small cubes
½ red onion, roughly chopped
1 teaspoon fine salt
1 teaspoon freshly ground black pepper
1 tablespoon extra virgin olive oil
½ red chilli/chile, deseeded and finely chopped
plain/all-purpose flour, for dusting the work surface
4 x ½ sprigs fresh rosemary, roughly broken up
plant-based milk, for glazing
1 tablespoon vegan balsamic vinegar glaze, store-bought or make your own (see below)

BALSAMIC VINEGAR GLAZE
4 tablespoons vegan balsamic vinegar
1 tablespoon maple syrup or agave syrup

11-cm/4-inch plain round cookie cutter
8-cm/3-inch plain round cookie cutter

Prepare the vegan rough puff pastry and chill as instructed.

Preheat the oven to 200°C/fan 180°C (400°F) Gas 6.

Mix together the sweet potatoes, onion, salt, pepper and oil in a roasting pan and roast in the preheated oven for 20 minutes, turning occasionally, until the potatoes are starting to brown and the onion is starting to caramelize. Take out of the oven and mix in the chopped chilli/chile. Leave to cool. Remove the pastry from the fridge 10 minutes before you want to use it so that it is soft enough to work with.

Cut the pastry in half and roll one half out on a lightly floured work surface to a thickness of about 0.5-cm/¼-inch. Use the 11-cm/4-inch cutter to cut out four circles (reserving the offcuts). Use the smaller 8 cm/3-inch round cutter to stamp out the middles from two of the circles, so you are left with two rings (the centres of the rings are offcuts). Place the two larger pastry circles on a non-stick baking sheet, brush the edges with water to help them stick and sit the pastry rings on top. These will be your tart cases. Gently knead the pastry offcuts together with the remaining pastry, roll out and then repeat the steps above to make two more.

Spoon the sweet potato filling into the centre of each tart. Nestle a broken half-sprig of rosemary into the filling of each. Brush the pastry with vegan milk. Refrigerate for 10 minutes.

Meanwhile, if making your own glaze, combine the vinegar and maple or agave syrup in a small saucepan. Bring to the boil, then simmer gently until reduced by half and syrup-like.

Preheat the oven to 200°C/fan 180°C (400°F) Gas 6.

Bake the tarts in the preheated oven for 20 minutes until lightly golden brown. Immediately drizzle the hot tarts with the balsamic reduction. They are delicious eaten warm or cold.

maple, pecan & carrot dream cake

Some days only a moist, fluffy, lightly spiced carrot cake will do! The addition of maple and pecan makes this cake impossible not to love.

DIFFICULTY 🥄🥄🥄🥄🥄   **SERVES 12–15**   **PREP TIME 2½ HOURS + CHILL TIME**   **BAKE TIME 45 MINUTES**

CARROT SPONGE

6 eggs

175 g/¾ cup plus 2 tablespoons caster/granulated sugar

175 g/¾ cup plus 2 tablespoons soft light brown sugar

375 ml/1⅔ cups vegetable oil

400 g/3 cups plain/all-purpose flour

4 teaspoons bicarbonate of soda/baking soda

4 teaspoons each ground cinnamon and mixed spice

2 teaspoons fine salt

450 g/1 lb. peeled and grated carrots

PECAN CRUMB

150 g/5½ oz. pecan halves

30 g/1 oz. soft light brown sugar

50 g/1¾ oz. maple syrup

TO ASSEMBLE

100 g/3½ oz. Digestive Crumb (see page 13)

1 x batch Cream Cheese Custard (see page 18)

½ x batch Light as a Feather Cake Buttercream (see page 16)

125 g/½ cup full-fat cream cheese

1½ teaspoons vanilla bean paste

3 x 20-cm/8-inch cake pans, greased and bases lined with greaseproof baking parchment

Preheat the oven to 190°C/fan 170°C (375°F) Gas 5.

Put the eggs, both sugars and the oil into a mixing bowl. Mix together with a hand-held electric whisk (or use a stand mixer with the whisk attachment) at a medium speed.

In a separate bowl, sift the flour, bicarbonate of soda/baking soda, cinnamon, mixed spice and salt together. Mix the dry ingredients and the grated carrots into the egg mixture.

Divide the cake batter between the three prepared pans and bake in the preheated oven for 45 minutes until the sponges spring back to the touch. Remove from the oven (leaving the oven on) and leave to cool in the pans.

For the pecan crumb, roast the pecans on a baking sheet in the preheated oven for 15–20 minutes until fragrant. Reserve 12 for decoration and blitz the rest to a crumb in a food processor with the soft light brown sugar and maple syrup.

Prepare the digestive crumb. Prepare the cream cheese custard, then the buttercream. Warm the cream cheese just to room temperature in the microwave in a short burst, then mix with the vanilla and fold gently into the buttercream.

Turn out the sponges and trim the tops flat, saving the scraps. Line the sides of one of the pans that you baked the sponges in with a double layer of greaseproof baking parchment, about 15 cm/6 inches high. Add the first sponge, then spoon over 50 g/5½ oz. buttercream in blobs, do the same with the cheese custard. Scatter over a third of the pecan crumb, then 3½ tablespoons of digestive crumb. Repeat for the next layer. Add the top layer and smooth the remaining buttercream over. Refrigerate for 1–2 hours.

Remove the cake pan and paper. Place 12 pecans around the top edge and sprinkle with the remaining pecan crumble and leftover crumbled carrot sponge between to decorate.

red velvet 'cup' cakes

These aren't so much cupcakes as cakes cooked in a cup! We only use
beetroot/beet powder to create our red velvet sponge, which can easily
brown when baked, but there is no danger of that with this cooking method!

DIFFICULTY | MAKES 8 | PREP TIME 30 MINUTES | COOK TIME 45–50 SECONDS

SPONGE
90 g/¾ stick unsalted butter,
    melted and cooled
1 UK large/US extra-large egg,
    at room temperature
90 g/scant ½ cup caster/
    granulated sugar
1 teaspoon vanilla extract
18 g/scant ¾ oz. beetroot/
    beet powder
2 teaspoons cocoa powder
110 ml/scant ½ cup sour cream
2 teaspoons baking powder
85 g/scant ⅔ cup plain/
    all-purpose flour

EASY CREAM CHEESE FROSTING
100 g/1 stick minus 1 tablespoon
    unsalted butter, softened
40 g/3¼ tablespoons caster/
    granulated sugar
2 teaspoons vanilla extract
235 g/generous 1 cup full-fat
    cream cheese
edible flowers, to decorate

*piping/pastry bag with a large
    star-shaped nozzle/tip
    (approx. 2.5-3-cm/1-1¼-inch)*
*8 microwaveable glass or ceramic
    mugs, approx. 6-cm/2½ inches in
    diameter and 10 cm/4 inches high*

Put the melted butter, egg, sugar and vanilla into a large bowl
and mix well with a wooden spoon. Mix in the beetroot/beet
powder and cocoa powder. Add the sour cream and mix in.
Finally, sift in the baking powder and flour and mix thoroughly.
Rest the mixture at room temperature for 10 minutes.

Divide the mixture evenly into the heatproof glasses or
mugs, about 60 g/2¼ oz. per cup, it should take up about a
third to half of your cup. Don't be tempted to overfill as these
sponges rise a lot! Level out the tops with the back of a spoon.

Cook 2 cups at a time in the microwave on maximum
power (900W) for 45–50 seconds, then leave to cool.
(If your microwave doesn't go that high, cook your sponges
for 10–15 seconds longer). Set aside to cool.

For the easy cream cheese frosting, put the butter, sugar
and vanilla in a mixing bowl. Beat with a hand-held electric
whisk (or use a stand mixer with the paddle attachment) until
light and fluffy, scraping down the bowl a few times. Mix the
cream cheese in slowly just for a few seconds. Make sure you
don't overmix as the frosting can become sloppy.

Put the frosting into the piping/pastry bag with the star-
shaped nozzle/tip. Pipe a large swirl on top of each sponge to
cover. Decorate with edible flower petals and serve with spoons.

blueberry & lemon cheesecake truffles

Blueberry cheesecake is an American favourite; here we combine those classic flavours with a splash of lemon, and the result is these total flavour bombs! Perfect with afternoon tea or as a sneaky treat.

DIFFICULTY · **MAKES 10–12** · **PREP TIME 45 MINUTES + CHILL TIME** · **BAKE TIME N/A**

200 g/7 oz. leftover vanilla cake sponge (or ½ batch 15-cm/ 6-inch Vanilla Cake Batter, see page 11)
200 g/7 oz. Digestive Crumb (see page 13)
60 g/2 oz. Blueberry Jam (see page 21)
1 teaspoon natural lemon extract
20 g/1½ tablespoons full-fat cream cheese
10 g/¼ oz. blueberry powder
100 g/3½ oz. white chocolate, melted

large plate or tray, lined with greaseproof baking parchment

Prepare the vanilla cake batter (if needed) and bake in one pan for 20–25 minutes. Prepare the digestive crumb, then the blueberry jam and leave both to cool.

Using your hands, finely crumble the cake sponge into a mixing bowl. Mix in the blueberry jam, lemon extract and cream cheese with a wooden spoon to form a dough-like mixture. Roll the mixture into 10–12 balls (the size of ping pong balls), then place on the prepared tray or plate and refrigerate for 30 minutes until firm.

In a food processor, blitz the digestive crumb with the blueberry powder. Dip each cake truffle into the melted white chocolate and turn to cover them completely, then roll in the blueberry crumb. Refrigerate again for 5–10 minutes until set.

These will last for a good week stored in an airtight container in the fridge.

nutella-stuffed cookies

Cookies are great, Nutella-stuffed cookies are even better! The addition of chopped roasted hazelnuts to the cookie mix intensifies the nutty flavour and adds an extra crunch against the soft, gooey centre. You can use the base to make other flavours, such as coconut stuffed with raspberry jam.

DIFFICULTY   **MAKES 12**   **PREP TIME 30 MINUTES**   **BAKE TIME 12 MINUTES**

250 g/2¼ sticks unsalted butter, softened
175 g/¾ cup plus 2 tablespoons caster/granulated sugar
175 g/¾ cup plus 2 tablespoons soft light brown sugar
2 eggs
2 teaspoons vanilla bean paste
500 g/3¾ cups plain/all-purpose flour
3 teaspoons fine salt
2 teaspoons baking powder
150 g/5½ oz. roughly chopped roasted hazelnuts
50 g/1¾ oz. dark/bittersweet chocolate chips
300 g/10½ oz. hazelnut chocolate spread, such as Nutella

2 baking sheets, lined with greaseproof baking parchment
disposable piping/pastry bag

Preheat the oven to 200°C/fan 180°C (400°F) Gas 6.

Put the butter and both sugars into a mixing bowl. Cream together at a medium speed with a hand-held electric whisk (or use the paddle attachment in a stand mixer) until light and fluffy. Add the eggs, one by one, mixing in after each addition. Mix in the vanilla bean paste.

Sift the flour, salt and baking powder into a separate bowl and stir in the chopped roasted hazelnuts and chocolate chips. Mix the dry ingredients into the butter, sugar and eggs to form a soft dough. Divide the dough mixture into 12 equal portions and roll into knobbly balls between your palms.

Put the hazelnut chocolate spread in the piping/pastry bag and snip off the tip to make a small hole. Flatten each ball of dough in the palm of your hand and pipe on a small ping pong ball-sized amount of hazelnut chocolate spread. Mould the dough back into a ball around the chocolate spread, making sure there are no gaps for it to leak.

Space the filled dough balls out on the prepared baking sheets with a 5-cm/2-inch gap either side, as they will spread.

Bake in the preheated oven for 12 minutes until puffed up with a slight browning at the edges. Transfer to a cooling rack and let cool before serving.

These cookies are perfect at any time of the day and are especially good with a cup of tea.

marathon runner biskies

This is an original biskie flavour which debuted at the Chelsea food market where we had our first stall. With salted caramel, chocolate and peanut butter, it's a winner!

DIFFICULTY 🥄🥄🥄🥄 **MAKES 12–15** | **PREP TIME 2½ HOURS + CHILL TIME** | **BAKE TIME 10–15 MINUTES**

CHOCOLATE BISKIE DOUGH

85 g/3 oz. Chocolate Crumb (see page 13)

125 g/1⅛ sticks unsalted butter, softened

70 g/⅓ cup plus 1 teaspoon caster/granulated sugar

70 g/⅓ cup soft light brown sugar

1 teaspoon baking powder

1 teaspoon fine salt

2 eggs, at room temperature

50 g/2½ tablespoons golden/light corn syrup

60 g/2¼ oz. milk chocolate, melted and cooled

140 g/1 cup plus 1 tablespoon plain/all-purpose flour

10 g/1¼ tablespoons cocoa powder

TO ASSEMBLE

150 g/5½ oz. Salted Caramel Sauce (see page 22)

1 x batch Biskie Buttercream (see page 16)

150 g/5½ oz. smooth peanut butter

100 g/3½ oz. milk chocolate

100 g/3½ oz. salted peanuts

15 chewy caramel candies

piping/pastry bag with a plain 2-cm/¾-inch nozzle/tip

Prepare the chocolate crumb and set aside to cool.

Put the butter, both sugars, baking powder and salt in a mixing bowl. Beat together at a medium speed using a hand-held electric whisk (or use a stand mixer with the paddle attachment) until light and fluffy.

Scrape down the bowl and add the eggs and golden/light corn syrup. Beat for 10 minutes at a medium speed until well combined – the mixture should resemble thick yogurt.

Add the cooled melted chocolate and chocolate crumb and sift in the flour and cocoa powder. Beat in slowly at first, then at a medium speed for 1–2 minutes until well combined. Pop the mixture into a container, cover with a lid and chill in the fridge for about 1 hour until firm.

Preheat the oven to 180°C/fan 160°C (350°F) Gas 4.

Scoop out 20 g/¾ oz. portions of the mixture. Roll into balls and space out over two non-stick baking sheets with 4-cm/1½-inch gaps each side. Bake in the preheated oven for 10–15 minutes until slightly darker. Let cool on a cooling rack.

Prepare the salted caramel and set aside. Prepare the biskie buttercream, add the peanut butter and mix well. Put the buttercream into the piping/pastry bag with the 2-cm/¾-inch nozzle/tip and pipe two rings, one on top of the other, on the flat side of half the biskies (the bases). Fill the centre of each with 2 teaspoons of caramel. Refrigerate for 20 minutes.

Meanwhile, melt the milk chocolate in a heatproof bowl in the microwave in short bursts and roughly chop the peanuts. Decorate the curved side of the remaining biskies (the tops) by drizzling with the melted milk chocolate. Place a few peanut pieces on top of each one and then a chewy caramel candy, using the chocolate to help them stick. Leave at room temperature for 10 minutes until the chocolate is set.

Gently place the top biskies on the bottom ones and serve.

cookie dough brownies

An incredible combination of fudgy brownie topped with sweet, salty, chewy cookie dough, this is another all-time customer favourite and best-selling bake for us. You can easily switch up the flavour of the cookie dough by adding nuts or fruit.

DIFFICULTY | **MAKES 9** | **PREP TIME 30 MINUTES** | **BAKE TIME 20–25 MINUTES**

BROWNIE BASE
40 g/3 tablespoons unsalted butter, diced
85 g/3 oz. dark/bittersweet chocolate, broken into pieces
160 g/¾ cup plus 1 tablespoon caster/granulated sugar
3 eggs
80 g/⅔ cup minus 1 tablespoon plain/all-purpose flour
40 g/generous ⅓ cup cocoa powder

COOKIE DOUGH
125 g/1⅛ sticks unsalted butter
250 g/1¾ cups plus 2 tablespoons plain/all-purpose flour
1 teaspoon fine salt
1 teaspoon baking powder
85 g/½ cup minus 1 tablespoon caster/granulated sugar
85 g/½ cup minus 1 tablespoon soft light brown sugar
100 g/3½ oz. dark/bittersweet chocolate chips
1 egg
1 teaspoon vanilla extract
50 g/1¾ oz. crispy chocolate-covered balls, such as Maltesers

23-cm/9-inch square baking pan, 5-cm/2-inches deep, lined with greaseproof baking parchment

Preheat the oven to 180°C/fan 160°C (350°F) Gas 4.

For the brownie base, melt the butter and chocolate in the microwave in short bursts until liquid. Leave to cool slightly.

Put the sugar and eggs into a mixing bowl. Whisk together with a hand-held electric whisk (or use a stand mixer with the whisk attachment) at a medium speed until light, thick and the mixture can hold a figure of eight. Slowly add the chocolate-butter to the egg mixture, whisking until combined.

Sift together the flour and cocoa powder and slowly mix in to the chocolate mixture until combined. Transfer the mixture to the prepared baking pan and spread out evenly.

Now make the cookie dough layer. Melt the butter and leave to cool. Meanwhile, sift the flour, salt and baking powder into a mixing bowl. Add the caster/granulated sugar, soft light brown sugar and the chocolate chips and stir by hand with a wooden spoon until evenly distributed. Add the egg, cooled melted butter and vanilla extract and mix until evenly combined. Spread the cookie dough on top of the brownie mixture as evenly as possible and sprinkle over the crispy chocolate-covered balls.

Bake in the preheated oven for 20–25 minutes until lightly golden but still wobbly in the centre.

Leave to cool completely in the pan before turning out and slicing into nine squares to serve.

chocolate, banana & caramel pie

Our family go crazy for this easy no-bake pie! The custard is rich
and chocolatey, but not too sweet, and is the perfect pairing with
the sweet bananas and caramel and fresh whipped cream.

DIFFICULTY | **SERVES 10–12** | **PREP TIME 45 MINUTES +** | **BAKE TIME N/A**
| | **CHILL TIME** |

BASE
125 g/1⅛ sticks unsalted butter
200 g/7 oz. Digestive Crumb
   (see page 13) or digestive
   biscuits/graham crackers,
   roughly broken
50 g/¼ cup demerara/
   turbinado sugar

TOPPING
½ x batch Caramel Sauce
   (see page 22)
1 x batch Chocolate Custard
   (see page 18)
3 medium ripe bananas
300 ml/1¼ cups double/heavy
   cream
a little dark/bittersweet chocolate,
   for grating over the top

*25-cm/10-inch pie dish or a 23-cm/
9-inch loose-based tart pan*

For the base, melt the butter and leave to cool completely.
Put the digestive crumb or digestive biscuits/graham cracker
pieces into a food processor with the cooled melted butter
and blitz to fine crumbs. Tip into a bowl, add the demerara/
turbinado sugar and mix well. The sugar adds a nice crunch.

Press the crumb mixture into the pie dish or tart pan to
cover the base and up the sides, then pop into the fridge for
15 minutes until the base is set.

Meanwhile, for the topping, prepare the caramel and leave
to cool slightly. Prepare the chocolate custard and leave to
cool completely.

Peel and slice the bananas into 5-mm/¼-inch slices and
mix together with the caramel. Spread the banana caramel
evenly over the bottom of the digestive/graham cracker base.
Pour over the chocolate custard and spread smooth with a
spatula. Leave the pie to set in the fridge for 1–2 hours or until
you are ready to serve.

When you want to finish the pie, whip the double/heavy
cream until medium-soft, so it just holds its shape. Spoon over
the pie and grate some dark/bittersweet chocolate over the
top to decorate. Serve.

crazy shakes

We created crazy shakes for a TV show that were filming an episode in our Soho store. Now we get so many customer requests!

250 ml/1 cup plus 1 tablespoon vanilla ice cream, plus 2 extra scoops
250 ml/1 cup plus 1 tablespoon cold whole milk
½ x batch Caramel Sauce (see page 22)
200 g/7 oz. Salted Caramel Brownies (see page 34), crumbled
2 large marshmallows, toasted with a cook's blowtorch or under the grill/broiler
white chocolate star sprinkles, to decorate

CHOCOLATE SAUCE
130 ml/generous ½ cup double/heavy cream
100 g/3½ oz. dark/bittersweet chocolate, broken into pieces

2 x mason/Kilner jars and 2 paper straws

MAKES 2 CRAZY SHAKES

To make the chocolate sauce, heat the cream until simmering in a small saucepan. Turn off the heat and add the chocolate. Stir until melted and smooth. Set aside until cool.

To make the milkshake, mix the ice cream with the milk until smooth and combined.

Place your mason/Kilner jars on serving plates and drizzle inside the jars with the chocolate sauce. Divide the milkshake between the two jars, filling almost to the top, then add another scoop of ice cream on the top of each. Drizzle over more chocolate sauce, then the caramel sauce. Sprinkle the crumbled brownies into the ice cream. Add a toasted marshmallow to each and some chocolate star sprinkles, as many as you desire (it's crazy after all). Add straws and serve.

hot chocolate

For us the perfect hot chocolate isn't powdery, too thick, too sweet or too rich! We have created a hot chocolate blend that is deliciously comforting and satisfying. Add a dash of salted caramel (see page 22) for an extra layer of decadence. Sit back and enjoy!

40 g/1½ oz. dark/bittersweet chocolate
40 g/1½ oz. milk chocolate
125 g/⅔ cup minus 2 teaspoons caster/granulated sugar
125 g/1¼ cups cocoa powder
200 ml/generous ¾ cup your favourite milk

SERVES 1

Finely grate the dark/bittersweet chocolate and milk chocolate and mix together with the sugar and cocoa powder in a bowl. (You can keep this hot chocolate mix for about 6 months in an airtight container in a cool place; it will make about 20 cups.)

To make one cupful, place 1½ tablespoons of the hot chocolate mix in a small saucepan with the milk over a low heat. Stir and warm through until steaming.

Pour into a mug and serve topped with a sprinkling of the hot chocolate mix, if you like.

afternoon tea
MENUS

You can mix and match the recipes in this book
to create your own bespoke afternoon tea menus.
Whether you want to celebrate an occasion, treat
someone special or bake just for fun, here are
some ideas to inspire you and get you started.

Eclectic mix

Mini Vegetable Spring Rolls
(see page 107)
Mango & Passion Fruit Biskies
(see page 119)
Miso Caramel Madeleines
(see page 112)
Lychee & Rose Lattes (see page 48)

Mother's day

Smoked Cheese & Black Pepper
Scones (see page 26)
Raspberry Ripple Layer Cake
(see page 91)
Lemon Treacle Tarts
(see page 83)
London Fog Tea (see page 101)

Quick and easy

Bacon & Sweetcorn Muffins
(see page 130)
Rock Cake Scones (see page 84)
Red Velvet 'Cup' Cakes (See page 141)
Raspberry, Lemon & Mint Iced Green
Tea (see page 48)

Kid's faves

Pizza Pastry Twists (see page 133)
Strawberry Cake Truffles
(see page 97)
Cookie Dough Brownies
(see page 149)
Ombre Rainbow Layer Cake
(see page 63)
Pink Lemonade (see page 101)

Perfect picnic

Pork, Stuffing & Cranberry Sausage
Rolls (see page 80)
Black Sesame Sandwich Cookies
(see page 115)
Salted Carmel Cake Truffles
(see page 47)
Passion Fruit, Lychee & Orange Iced
Tea (see page 127)

Vegan delights

Roasted Sweet Potato Tarts
(see page 136)
Curry Puffs (see page 104)
Toffee Apple Cupcakes (see page 94)
Cauldron Cupcakes (see page 69)
Aquafaba Pavlovas (see page 98)

Showstopper celebration

'Rose' Courgette Tartlets
(see page 52)
Yuzu & Lemon Egg Custard Tart
(see page 116)
Chocolate & Salted Caramel Heaven
Cake (see page 41)
Pearl Biskies (see page 66)
Unicorn Sours (see page 73)

Sweet-tooth heaven

Marathon Runner Biskies
(see page 146)
Coconut Dream Cake (see page 123)
Apple Pie Mousse with Shortbread
Bows (see page 59)
Freakshakes (see page 153)

Rainbow treats

Feta & Red Pepper Pinwheel Scones
(see page 55)
Matcha & Strawberry Melting
Moments (see page 120)
Ombre Rainbow Layer Cake
(see page 63)
Galaxy Juice (see page 73)

Emily & Annabel's dream afternoon tea

Mini Sweetcorn Pancakes
(see page 30)
Creamy Leek & Potato Pies
(see page 79)
Maple, Pecan & Carrot Dream Cake
(see page 137)
Strawberries & Cream Biskies
(see page 33)
Chocolate Banana & Caramel Pie
(see page 150)

index

acknowledgements

A massive high five to the amazing people that have made this book possible: Tamara, Clare and Alex for bringing our recipes to life and making them look so gorgeous. Megan, Alice and the team at RPS for their guidance and support to us newbie authors.

To our family, thank you for being everything from delivery drivers, to market stall hands, construction contractors and business mentors. IT support, brawn, taste testers (okay, it was our fault you put on weight!), crockery finders and the voice of 'hell no' in our moments of madness – you guys rock and you are the reason we are who we are and can do what we do.

To our friends who have stuck by and supported us in sun, rain, hail and snow-covered markets, helped us paint and decorate, make boxes and pitched in with all manner of random tasks! To John of Partridges, Chelsea, for taking a chance on two girls and a weird cookie-cake sandwich.

To our amazing teams at Cutter & Squidge, past, current and future, for helping us execute our vision and believing in us and our ethos. For the long days and hectic weeks, the laughter, blood, sweat and tears, you will always be part of our Cutter & Squidge family.